Mentoring Young Men of Color

Mentoring Young Men of Color

Meeting the Needs of African American and Latino Students

HORACE R. HALL

Rowman & Littlefield Education
Lanham, Maryland • Toronto • Oxford
2006

Published in the United States of America
by Rowman & Littlefield Education
A Division of Rowman & Littlefield Publishers, Inc.
A wholly owned subsidiary of The Rowman & Littlefield Publishing Group, Inc.
4501 Forbes Boulevard, Suite 200, Lanham, Maryland 20706
www.rowmaneducation.com

PO Box 317
Oxford
OX2 9RU, UK

British Library Cataloguing in Publication Information Available

Library of Congress Cataloging-in-Publication Data

Hall, Horace R.
　Mentoring young men of color : meeting the needs of African American and
Latino students / Horace R. Hall.
　　p.　cm.
　ISBN-13: 978-1-57886-429-4 (hardcover : alk. paper)
　ISBN-10: 1-57886-429-1 (hardcover : alk. paper)
　ISBN-13: 978-1-57886-430-0 (pbk. : alk. paper)
　ISBN-10: 1-57886-430-5 (pbk. : alk. paper)
　1. African American teenage boys–Education.　2. Hispanic American teenage
boys–Education.　3. Mentoring in education–United States.　I. Title.
　LC2731.H35　2006
　373.1829'96073–dc22
2006000651

♾ ™ The paper used in this publication meets the minimum requirements of
American National Standard for Information Sciences—Permanence of
Paper for Printed Library Materials, ANSI/NISO Z39.48-1992.
Manufactured in the United States of America.

To
Robert "Sunshine" Agusto and Samuel Kingston Hall—
my mentor and mentee

Contents

Preface

In many respects, the ideas expressed in *Mentoring Young Men of Color: Meeting the Needs of African American and Latino Students* transcend conventional notions of mentoring as purely a one-on-one, out-of-school endeavor. While adhering to some of the more general descriptions of the practice (e.g., a nurturing relationship between a wise and trusted, nonrelated adult and a young person), many of the concepts presented here can be directly translated into the classroom environment, empowering both students and teachers. Conversely, for those deeply engaged in mentoring, this work also presents multiple strategies for promoting youth development, as well as preventing youth problems in and outside of the school setting.

Mentoring Young Men of Color is not solely about challenging contemporary perceptions of males of color as wholly problematic. This work is also intended to serve as a viable advocate for all youth—those young people who rarely, if ever, participate in boardrooms or policy-making forums where impassive decisions are made to control their lives and decide their fate. *Mentoring Young Men of Color* is about looking at young people from different perspectives, seeing past their anti-social behavior, and looking deeper into the causes of their actions. It is about discovering how to reach and make a difference in the life of a child, if only just one.

The current path that our nation is taking—increased zero tolerance policies, strengthened legal actions against youth, and the relentless construction of more state prisons—is not the answer. Young people are not simply a number or someone's property. Youth need to know that they are wanted, that they can make a difference, that they are loved, and that we hold their best interests at heart. The more love they receive, the more love they will give. I hope that this work reaches other caring youth workers and community members, locally, nationally, and abroad, who struggle to understand, educate, connect with, and bring justice to the lives of young people. We cannot turn our backs on them. They represent the future—our future.

There is no American population more misperceived, more misjudged, and more misunderstood than children and adolescents. From the basic foundation of the home and community to our country's vast public school and legal system, youth are caught in an emotional, social, physical, and psychological maelstrom. Their voices are largely ignored in the worlds they inhabit, and their images are distorted by mass media and the powers that be. Adolescent males of color, in particular, are frequently characterized by various media forms as predatory, villainous, and bestial. Consequently, America's perception of these young men not only negatively influences the way social systems deal with them, but also how they, in turn, relate to themselves. Many become self-loathing, dismissive, despondent, and indifferent to the world around them.

One supportive measure to aid these young men in overcoming the landslide of hurtful imagery and feelings that engulf their lives is youth mentoring. The positive influence of an older individual in the lives of young people has a long, documented history. Yet, over the past several decades, there has been a renewed interest in youth mentoring given present-day circumstances: suspected rising youth crime, heightened zero tolerance school policies, and troubled teens becoming increasingly withdrawn, silenced, and angry. With this, multitudes of youth mentoring programs have surfaced nationally and abroad in school districts, businesses, community organizations, and government agencies. Their main objective is to prepare young people for success in adult life. While most programs attempt to support children and adolescents labeled as "at-risk," "troubled," or "problematic," others focus on those deemed as gifted, motivated, or high-achieving. *Mentoring Young Men of Color* looks at the phenomenon of youth mentoring through a cultural lens. This work not only investigates the value of school-based mentoring in the lives of adolescent males of color but also offers alternative, more positive ways in which our society can experience and embrace this social group. Understanding mentoring as a cultural practice, *Mentoring Young Men of Color* informs schools and communities of the roles and responsibilities that they have in fighting the public assault on America's youth and helping young males of color see themselves as redeemable and fully human.

Originally based on a study of an urban youth mentoring program, this book presents a critical viewpoint of the social realties that Latino and African American adolescent boys grapple with on a daily basis. The work takes a serious look at how educational, cultural, and social factors exert a profound influence upon the success and failure of this student population. This perspective illuminates the everyday institutional practices of schools and how they, in effect, add to the discontent and disillusion of young males of color.

In recent years, a plethora of handbooks, manuals, and reports on mentoring have been the subject of increased attention. Although many of these publications offer readers the benefits of mentoring partnerships, organizational strategies for programs, and approaches to healthy child development, they provide little to no recommendation on how to assist youth of color in deconstructing, as well as counteracting, society's misperception and negative treatment of them. Moreover, these materials are largely devoid of curriculum and in-school activities that serve to assist young males of color in releasing pent-up anxiety and emotion.

Other publications, not necessarily based on mentoring but focusing on relationships with boys, have also been a center of much interest. For example, W. S. Pollack's *Real Boys' Voices* and Ann A. Ferguson's *Bad Boys* each take an extensive and meaningful look into adolescent male issues: gender construction, racial profiling, homophobia, male violence, and academic disidentification. Pollack's work utilizes young male voices, while Ferguson presents critical analysis and practical advice for readers working with African American boys in the school environment.

Mentoring Young Men of Color represents a combination of approaches. It is a guide into the social, emotional, and academic world of young males of color, while also serving as an informational handbook on practical mentoring and teaching methods. The book builds on the work of Pollack and Ferguson by exploring the everyday problems adolescent males of color face (e.g., teacher bias, rigid school policies, dysfunctional home life, street and gang violence), discussing how these phenomena impact their lives, and offering viable strategies to assist mentors, teachers, and youth workers. The discussions presented in this work help explain why mentoring is a vital source for inner-city youth, what flaws exist in classrooms and administrative practices in reaching males of color, why student culture needs to be a more integral part of classroom curriculum, and how mentoring programs can help bridge gaps between schools and the immediate community.

Mentoring Young Men of Color also advances existing research on mentoring by redefining conventional ideals and notions of what it is. This book argues that, equal to providing younger individuals with wisdom and insight into how to be successful, mentoring must engage youth in defining what success is for them personally. Mentoring practices can no longer focus on imposing a particular way of being on young people, whether socially, culturally, or economically, if it is not realistic to their lives.

Because children and adolescents come from a range of situations and backgrounds, mentors must recognize the spaces that young people occupy, give them options that exist outside their present conditions, and assist them in being authors of their own destiny. Ultimately, it is they who must decide on and execute positive change as they see fit. As mentors, we are simply there to inform and support them in this transformative process. In short, we must meet them where they are.

The audience for this book includes scholars and students of education, sociology, psychology, and social work, as well as those concerned with curriculum design, school counseling, classroom management, and community development. Teacher educators will find this book particularly useful for those undergraduate and graduate courses related to the philosophy and psychology of children and adolescents, the multicultural classroom, culture and education, leadership practices for urban administrators, and designing and interpreting curriculum. Written in an engaging and accessible language, this book encourages extensive dialogue related to the relevance and essentialism of school-based mentoring as it speaks to both student and community advocacy.

Additionally, *Mentoring Young Men of Color* evokes classroom thought and discussion on a broad range of other educational issues including:

- academic disidentification and student drop out,
- youth violence prevention,
- diverse values and voices within the classroom,
- the importance of arts-based curriculum,
- socially and culturally responsive education,
- critical urban pedagogy, and
- student empowerment and agency.

Discourse surrounding these themes may compel practitioners, policymakers, social scientists, and curriculum designers to play a constructive role in creating and implementing a standard for such programmatic endeavors that involve school-based mentoring.

Mentoring Young Men of Color balances the conceptual with the practical, the theoretical with the reflective, and the psychological with the logical. This body of work serves to expand our consciousness, while enlightening both scholarship and community to the less-understood lives of young males of color. Throughout this book, readers are presented with a range of classroom activities and recommendations that serve to enrich mentoring and teaching practices and enhance one's perception of students of color. This work is critical urban pedagogy in theory and in action. It serves to bring equity, empathy, and social justice to not only our schools and classrooms but to our communities as well.

The prologue, "Endangered?," is a discussion on the social and legal responses (e.g., increased zero tolerance policies, rising youth litigation, incarceration) immediate to the perception of escalating youth crime and violence in the United States. Media stories that racially profile Latino and African American males are highlighted, as well as social policies like that of zero tolerance.

Chapter 1, "Youth Mentoring: A View through Multiple Lenses," presents an overview of mentoring describing multiple definitions, types, purposes, and benefits. Particular attention is paid to two main forms of mentoring: school-based mentoring (SBM) programs and community-based mentoring (CBM) programs. This chapter also discusses one of the primary challenges faced by youth mentoring programs—mentor availability.

Chapter 2, "Embracing Young Males of Color in the School Domain," focuses specifically on the in-school barriers males of color struggle against: discipline issues, socially and culturally irrelevant curriculum, and their own lack of personal accountability. In this chapter, the Act of Removal is defined and discussed as being a prerequisite for successful school-based mentoring and classroom teaching and learning. Utilizing this concept in schools provides students with an active voice in classroom activities and projects.

Chapter 3, "Constructing a Space for Boys," looks at the role of school-based mentors working with adolescent males. A section is also dedicated to the role of SBM curriculum. Several models are introduced, including arts-based activities, reflective writing, conflict resolution, and social and culturally relevant discussion topics. The concept of brotherhood is also discussed as a by-product of an all-male forum.

Chapter 4, "Extending beyond a Space for Boys," explores ways of providing boys with a sense of empowerment and personal agency by taking them and their creative artwork beyond the four walls of the school. In addition, this chapter looks at the role SBM programs play in bridging social gaps between teachers and students and school and home life. This chapter reiterates the main points from the previous chapters, emphasizing the importance of SBM programs, the promise and potential they hold in assisting males of color, and benefits of planning and implementing such programmatic endeavors in classrooms and communities.

Chapter 5, "A REAL History Lesson Part 1: Origins of an SBM Program, is the first part of a brief history on the origin and development of an SBM youth program entitled REAL (Respect, Excellence, Attitude, and Leadership). This chapter looks at how and why the program was conceived, its initial curriculum format, and its subsequent pilot run.

Chapter 6, "A REAL History Lesson Part 2: A Quest for Realness," illustrates the lessons learned from the pilot run and how program curriculum was evaluated and altered to meet more of the individual needs of students. This section also describes the successes and failures in establishing a grassroots SBM program.

Chapter 7, "REAL Profiles: Mentors and Mentees," presents interviews from several of the REAL mentors and mentees who are featured in chapters 5 and 6. These participants reflect on their personal experiences with the program and their perception of its impact.

REFERENCES

Ferguson, A. A. (2001) *Bad Boys: Public Schools in the Making of Black Masculinity.* Ann Arbor: University of Michigan Press.

Pollack, W. S. (2000) *Real Boys' Voices.* New York: Random House.

Acknowledgments

There are so many people to thank for their assistance and guidance in this project. Mere words will never be able to express my true appreciation for the time and feelings shared with everyone. With that, allow me to make some attempt.

First and foremost, I would like to praise the most High for making this book, as well as all things, possible. I continue to walk by faith and not by sight.

Endless amounts of love and gratitude go to my wife, Samantha, and my mother, Elaine. They are the guiding angels in my life. Without their words of encouragement, strength, and kisses, I am not quite sure how my life would be. I love you both endlessly.

Special thanks go to all the members of the REAL Youth Program, as well as those who were not necessarily members but gave their time and support. Big ups to a few comrades in particular: Chiquita Agusto, Juan Bahena, Paris Brandy, Steven "MP" Callen, Nancy Castro, Alex Correa, Anthony Garcia, Tremaine Gunn, John Hackney Jr., Andre Huff, Anthony Lowe, Jairo Martinez, Larry Nash, Jorge Olea, Pam "Mocha Sista" Osbey, Zardon Richardson, Cleo Rodgers, Tony Romeo, Dave Stovall, Brenda Torres, and Alex Trakas.

To my university colleagues—William Ayers, Sharon Coleman, Jennifer DeLago, Mariaelena Donias-Rodriguez, Sharon Earthley, Marietta Giovanelli, Donald Hellison, Carol Melnick, José Perales, Jim Rowan, William Schubert, William Watkins, and Mark "Pickle" Wodziak—I have leaned on you all as either a graduate student or a professor. Your support and generosity brought balance to my life. You have my deepest gratitude.

Finally, I would like to thank my publisher, Rowman & Littlefield Education, particularly Tom Koerner, Cindy Tursman, Paul Cacciato, and Sally Craley. Their understanding of the need and significance of mentoring in the lives of youth of color helped to transform my manuscript into the kind of work that genuinely seeks to enlighten and inspire a wider audience.

Prologue: Endangered?

The color of violence is black.
Those are the facts, spread eagled
Against a white background,
Where policemen have cornered the enemy,
Where he shouldn't be, which is seen.

—AI, "Endangered Species"

There is a recurring phrase in the scholarly and research literature that refers to Latino and African American males as an "endangered species." I often think with a kind of simmering horror how objectifying it is to refer to members of our human race and experience as endangered, as if they could somehow be forced into the same category as the Siberian tiger or the humpback whale.

Endangered? Perhaps not biologically, although Latino and African American males, as opposed to their white counterparts, suffer from shorter life spans, higher mortality rates, and poorer quality of health. From a sociological perspective, males of color* can surely be viewed as being under siege. They run greater risks of negative treatment from

*Throughout this book, "males of color" will specifically refer to males within African American, Hispanic, and Chicano ethnic groups. "People of color," in general, is an inclusive category including African, Asian, Latino, Native American, and third-world people.

1

teachers and law enforcement agents, particularly after the childhood years when their once-perceived cuteness and innocent frivolity is now seen as disruptive, menacing, and even violent behavior. As they journey into adulthood, these young men begin to see themselves as targets of discrimination and punishment at school, at work, and in their own communities.

The frequently used expression "endangered species" as a metaphor to describe the present condition of males of color speaks to our perceptions, or rather our misperceptions, of this population. Without question, this social group faces dire circumstances both socially and physically. However, the damaging imagery surrounding such rhetoric implies that males of color are entities separate from our world community and that their possible "extinction" would have no bearing upon our shared human existence.

The trappings of such language fosters a kind of social consciousness whereby we begin to perceive males of color as objects that have no real connection to our collective human thread. As a consequence, these males have internalized their objectification, leading to feelings of isolation from not just the educational system but also from society at large. This disconnect can be seen in their underachievement in school, their expressions of anger and violence toward others, and their self-annihilation through drug and alcohol abuse. Regrettably, our society's overwhelming response to their reality has been to literally and figuratively lock them up and throw away the key.

BLACK AND BROWN YOUTH CRIME: DAILY NEWS OR DAILY HYPE?

Within American society, the general public is inundated with a deluge of information that understandably skews their perceptions of males of color. Newspapers, magazines, and nightly news segments across the United States frequently spotlight Latino and African American youth as perpetrators of violent crimes in our nation's inner cities. The distorted nature of these reports generates the false perception that crime, committed by these young people, is escalating at alarming rates. As a result, laws and statutes, at both the local and national level, have been created to curb this ostensible increase.

For instance, in 1994 California adopted the Three Strikes law, which serves as a prosecutorial-based, mandatory sentencing law primarily focused on sharply penalizing recidivist offenders. In that same year, President Clinton signed the Gun-Free Schools Act, requiring states to put expulsion policies into effect for students bringing firearms to school. By June 1996, all fifty states were in compliance with this law. In 2000, Proposition 21 was passed by California voters, allowing prosecutors to initiate adult charges against juveniles for relatively minor drug and property crimes. The proposition lowers the age at which teenagers can start accruing the "strikes" that could ultimately result in a life sentence under the state's "three strikes and you're out" statutes.

As legal actions against youth have continued to reveal themselves in communities across America, increased juvenile arrests have followed. This, in turn, has multiplied court caseloads, with inadequate legal representation for juveniles as a consequence. Between 1992 and 1997, legislatures in forty-seven states and the District of Columbia ratified laws that allowed the transfer of youth from the juvenile justice system to the criminal justice system. The result has been a dramatic increase of juvenile populations in adult prisons. What is crucial to observe here is that a disproportionate number of youth of color are being represented in the judicial system. The growth in juvenile arrests, as well as the rise in admission and population of detention centers, correctional facilities (e.g., training schools, camps, and ranches), and adult prisons, mainly comprises nonwhite offenders.

Undeniably, through such legal sanctions, racial profiling abounds. In point of fact, African American youth only make up 15 percent of all young people in this nation, yet they occupy 65 percent of all bed space in detention facilities. Forty-nine percent of all juveniles arrested for violent offenses are African American, and 52 percent of all children who are transferred to stand trial, as adults, are African American. Latino and Native American youth make up 60 percent of the children prosecuted in the adult federal system. The irony is that higher rates of recidivism have been thought to occur in part because young offenders not only find themselves sharing a cell with an adult offender, but they also find a role model there. In this arrangement, negative behaviors may be reinforced and perpetuated.

Over the past several years, we have also witnessed an upsurge of legal actions in our school systems in the form of zero tolerance policies. Although the 1994 Gun-Free Schools Act mainly focused on the brandishing of firearms, some states have gone well beyond this law by suspending and expelling students for carrying virtually any object or posing any sort of physical threat in the school environment. For instance, weekly suspensions have included a seven-year-old for bringing nail clippers to school, a fourth-grader who forgot his belt and broke the school dress code, a fifteen-year-old for dying his hair blue, the arrest of a thirteen-year-old male student who spent five days in jail for writing a story about killing his classmates, and the suspension of an eight-year-old for pointing a breaded chicken finger at a teacher and saying, "Pow, pow, pow!"

Opponents of zero tolerance policies claim that such harsh responses are based on the assumption, held by 62 percent of all Americans, that school and youth violence is increasing at an intolerable rate. Yet, according to the 2003 Uniform Crime Reports in the United States, all categories of juvenile crimes have been on the decline and juvenile homicides have dropped a significant 30 percent since 1993. In spite of this decrease, zero tolerance policies, in our streets and schools, continue to cast a broad net over violators, regardless of the severity of offense.

Oddly, there are virtually no data to indicate that zero tolerance policies minimize school violence. In fact, some research proposes that certain tactics, like strip searches, the use of metal detectors, and undercover police officers in schools, can produce emotional harm, increase student distrust of authority figures, and influence students to drop out. The irony of zero tolerance policies is that in their blind efforts to mitigate school violence, they create and perpetuate a form of systemic violence vis-à-vis suspension and expulsion. School suspension has consistently been a moderate-to-strong predictor of student dropout. Preventing one access to a formal educational experience is an act of violence within itself. In contrast to the media's overrepresentation of young males of color as perpetrators of urban violence, what must not be overlooked is the fact that children and adolescents have a higher rate of victimization than adults in both rural and urban areas. It is important to note that youth are the most highly victimized segment of the U.S. population. This reality often goes unnoticed as victimization data is reported in a way that does not contrast the experiences of adults and youth. Despite this higher occurrence of youth victimization, young males of color in particular are still stigmatized as criminal, violent, sexually deviant, and a threat to themselves and to the broader society.

As a nation, we have typically responded to the delinquent acts of young males of color through punitive measures, while paying very little attention to structural disadvantages. Root factors such as residential segregation, illiteracy, poverty, and racism negatively impact the quality of family and peer life. Thus, we find many inner-city youth living through the everyday environmental and psychological pressures of low economic status, home and community violence, joblessness, fatherlessness, and even lovelessness.

Observing the U.S. Latino population, one in every four Latino families and almost two in five Latino children live in poverty. In fact, 60 percent of this population reports an annual income that places them well below the federal poverty level. Homicide has been inversely connected with the level of income among Mexican- and Puerto Rican-born males. The disproportionate number of Latinos living in impoverished urban centers places them at a higher risk than non-Latinos.

By looking closer at the impact of structural disadvantages, we can also see that much of the violence perpetrated by urban youth with firearms or other weapons occurs primarily on an interpersonal or intercultural basis, also referred to as youth-on-youth or black-on-black crime. In other words, the anger and discontent that some of these young men harbor is largely being vented within their own homes and neighborhoods. Thus, the victims of their aggressive acts are those who reside in the immediate community: mothers, fathers, sisters, brothers, husbands, wives, teachers, and, without question, the young perpetrators themselves.

Structural disadvantages also have a negative influence on schooling experiences. Academic underachievement, failure, and dropout for urban youth of color have been associated with a decline in parental involvement, a lack of male teachers and role models, increased exposure to violent situations, negative attitudes toward their minority status, and low self-esteem. These dynamics, combined with a turbulent home life, limited community resources (e.g., youth organizations, athletic groups, violence prevention programs), and the disintegration of the traditional family unit, unquestionably influence children's behavioral and cognitive development, leading to the antisocial, aggressive, and even violent behaviors evident in many of today's youth.

Similar to the pejorative connotation that the term "endangered species" places upon males of color, laws and policies promoting zero tolerance are clearly manufactured by our perceptions of this social group. When we perceive youth as dangerous, confrontational, and out of control, we are ready to respond with tactics of control. We quickly label them, classify them, and, in some cases, lock them away. To make it plain, our perceptions guide our actions.

With all intent and urgency, we must abandon our obsession with discipline-and-punish-style methods as long-term reducers of aggressive and antisocial behaviors. These young people require the same energy, attention, and resources that have been accorded to the problem of reprimanding them. Implemented as more of a preventive measure, alternative approaches like school- and community-based mentoring may hold the key to connecting with young males of color in more effective and sensitive ways.

Considering the slanted depictions of young males of color in the news media, the mistreatment that they face in schools and in the larger society, the rising number of youth incarcerated annually, and the extreme penalties that *all* young people are experiencing in nearly every segment of our society, we can see that the metaphor of "endangered species" is more than a singular, ethnic predicament. When this metaphor is used to solely classify males of color, we must be aware of the myopic vision that such language creates and that at its core lies shared human responsibility. By creating a wider lens to see individuals, we can experience them more completely, learning to draw connections between them and ourselves.

Mentoring Young Men of Color is about taking time to understand the uniqueness and diversity of male students of color rather than judging them based on their parts. Taking time is a process that demands us to break away from the skewed images and representations that envelop this group; it is a practice that requires us to provide them with recognition, empowerment, and agency, largely in cases where their voices are silenced and their identities are marginalized. It is a selfless act that asks us to embrace these males despite their outward indifference, rebelliousness, or anger. When we take time, we afford ourselves the opportunity to develop genuine relationships with these young people, whereby we as adults can serve as lifelong supporters of their dreams, visions, and goals. In short, we become engaged in youth mentoring.

Our true success as mentors, teachers, parents, school counselors, administrators, community workers, and policymakers hinges on our ability to effectively peel back the layers of these young peoples' lives and render a more honest picture that shows them as delicate and redeemable. We cannot authentically connect with their hearts and souls if somewhere resting in the back of our minds is an ominous image of who we think they are. We must come to see our classrooms, schools, and communities as made up of individuals with separate, as well as identical, needs, issues, and concerns. Without delay, we must aspire to hear and see these young males more clearly, to know that they hold promise and have infinite value.

1

Youth Mentoring: A View through Multiple Lenses

You often say, "I would give, but only to the deserving."
The trees in your orchard say not so, nor the flocks in your
pasture.
They give that they may live, for to withhold is to perish.

—Kahlil Gibran, *The Prophet*

For generations, mentoring has been planned and implemented in a wide range of arenas: schools, homes, churches, community organizations, business offices, and the Internet. While operational definitions of mentoring vary from program to program, it is typically considered to be a relationship where a person with greater experience assists another with less. This relationship is generally viewed as a one-on-one interaction of unrelated (non–blood relation) individuals of different ages networking on a regular basis.

Mentoring relationships usually take place over a fixed period of time. Some may extend over a school semester, while others can go on for months or even years depending on the function and purpose of the mentor–mentee involvement. However long the connection lasts, this form of social interaction embodies a reciprocal nature that enables both parties to contribute and learn from each other.

In the *classical model* of mentoring, the older, more experienced mentor supports the younger, less experienced mentee by concentrating on such facets as personal responsibility, professional advancement, positive character development, and/or the inculcation of social and cultural values. The overall objective is to serve as a professional helper or role model, providing the mentee with the necessary information and skills needed for successful living. This particular model is seen as more of a teacher–student relationship, and hence does not rely on an emotional connection in order to be functional.

When mentoring practices solely focus on children and adolescents, aspects of the classical model are normally expanded upon. The underlying goal of this aspect of mentoring is to improve the various dimensions of young people's lives (e.g., academic achievement, self-esteem, social competency, and resiliency) while connecting them to an individual from the school or community. Given that mentors are involved with youth on multiple levels, they often have to wear a variety of hats in order to connect: guide (teaching youth life skills and how to navigate various life circumstances), tutor (helping students with their studies), advocate (speaking up for young people where their voices are silenced), and friend (just being there to listen to needs, issues, and concerns).

Youth mentoring generally relies on a level of emotional engagement. As such, there are two basic types of mentor–mentee interactions that reflect different levels of involvement. The first interaction finds the mentor and mentee sharing a type of kinship, with the mentor becoming like an aunt or uncle. These mentors are consistently active in the life of their mentees and are usually familiar with family, friends, and teachers. It is the kind of relationship that has been established over a significant period of time and is emotionally open and committed.

The second mentor–mentee interaction is fairly less involved than the first. The mentor spends a lesser amount of time with the mentee and is not as emotionally invested. As opposed to being viewed as a quasi-family member, mentors of this second interaction are positioned in more of a friend-like role. They are not entirely aware of the day-to-day experiences of the mentee, nor are they as familiar with family, friends, or teachers. Despite this decreased level of intimacy, these mentors are still able to serve as an advocate, tutor, or guide. Through open and consistent communication, mentor–mentee friendships of this nature can be formed and sustained.

COMMUNITY-BASED AND SCHOOL-BASED MENTORING PROGRAMS

Mentoring programs are generally aimed at helping underserved youth cope with adverse social and economic circumstances that place them in "at-risk" or "endangered" categories. Now more than ever, young people are finding themselves detached from deteriorating family structures that no longer provide them with adequate guidance, discipline, or love. Outside of the family and home, academically struggling schools are being placed on the chopping block, forcing numbers of young people out of their schools and out of their education. Moreover, scarce community resources are leaving neighborhoods powerless in providing children and adolescents with sufficient outlets for healthy human development and growth.

Over the past twenty years there has been a virtual explosion of youth programs that claim mentoring as either the primary focus of their work or one of many modes of intervention. A majority of youth mentoring programs, depending on the needs of their target population, implement curriculum centered on academics, social competency, moral development, life skills, citizenship, arts-based education, health education, child rearing, and vocational and career training.

National programs like Big Brothers/Big Sisters of America (BIGS) and the National Mentoring Partnership, as well as more localized programs like Project 2000 (Washington, D.C.) and the Mentor/Mentee (M&M) program (Arkansas), promote the following:

- developing mentor–mentee relationships;
- strengthening student self-concept, character, and competence;
- increasing academic performance;
- developing mentee's behavioral and emotional dimensions;
- integrating mentors into school and home life;

- presenting adolescents with career goal opportunities; and
- networking with peers from different cultural backgrounds.

In addition to the above goals, there are smaller, less recognized youth mentoring programs whose curriculum focuses on race and ethnic identity, sexual minority adolescents (gay and lesbian), rites of passage, the creation and promotion of student-made products, and socially and culturally relevant issues related to social justice, democracy, and antiracism. Despite diversity in curriculum, youth mentoring generally seeks to bolster young people's self-esteem, advance their knowledge and skills, and expand their social networks.

Youth mentoring programs operate in either a one-to-one or group format. Many programs use the traditional community-based mentoring (CBM) approach, which brings a mentor and a mentee together one-on-one. Interactions generally take place on the weekends for a structured number of hours and within the community. Matching mentors with mentees is usually based on race, cultural background, shared economic status, life experiences, spoken language, and gender. In the one-on-one arrangement, adults are intensely screened, as much of their time with a young person is unsupervised.

CBM programs have proven to be beneficial for those youngsters taking part in them. Both children and adolescents in one-on-one relationships have been recognized as less likely to participate in the following behaviors: using illegal drugs, using alcohol, skipping school, engaging in violence. Additionally, this form of mentoring has also been proven to assist young people in building self-esteem and a sense of connectedness with their school, peers, and family, as well as minimizing at-risk behaviors by providing them with prosocial and empowering opportunities.

An increasingly popular option to the CBM model is school-based mentoring (SBM). This approach is usually less expensive than traditional programs, which can cost up to two or three times as much. The reason behind their cost-effectiveness is that SBMs, and the schools they partner with, typically share classroom space, photocopying and travel expenses, audio-video equipment, staff assistance, and so forth.

SBM programs are not only viewed as influential for career development but also as a salient factor in creating significant experiences for students while they are there in the school building. Given that students spend a large portion of their day in this learning environment, SBM is able to reach large groups of young people within a singular space and time. Such programs provide youth with safe and supervised surroundings where they can experience a sense of belonging through peer support and interaction. It is through the SBM approach that students learn not only how to operate in the interpersonal world but also how to work together to develop strategies for dealing with their academic and personal issues.

The SBM model also presents adults with the opportunity of carving out a portion of time to share with children and adolescents. Perhaps their weekends are busy, but during the week they are able to volunteer to work with an SBM program at a local area school. Being that SBMs generally work as a group dynamic, these volunteer adults are able to connect with greater numbers of youth at one specific time. With volunteer shortage being a widespread problem in mentoring programs, SBM or group mentoring compensates for the lack of adult availability and resources. As opposed to being preoccupied with recruitment and personnel strain, SBM programs use one or more mentors to serve small or large numbers of students.

Finally, SBM programs offer students with additional adult support in the school environment. Even the most dedicated teacher or administrator is unable to reach every student. With this in mind, SBMs are able to network with school staff and assist them in pinpointing those students who may need extra attention. For the student participating in the SBM, the end result can mean an enhanced feeling of belonging, higher academic achievement, a broadening of classroom knowledge, increased self-identification, and decreased levels of delinquency or violence.

MENTORS: A SHORTAGE OR A HIDDEN SUPPLY?

As previously mentioned, mentoring programs are frequently confronted by the enormous barrier of a limited number of adults who are able, or even willing, to volunteer their time as a mentor. Reasons for their lack of involvement vary: some adults are overwhelmed by their own family responsibilities; some are often restricted by long, hectic work hours; others would prefer to be paid for their participation. Whatever the issue, programs are continually faced with the difficulty of finding adults who are willing to contribute their time to young people in either the school or neighborhood setting. This crucial issue is one of the more prominent challenges faced by youth mentoring programs.

A key factor that weighs in heavily on the involvement of adults in mentoring programs is the selection procedure. The rule of thumb for most mentoring programs is to have adults provide reference checks and undergo a formal interview. This helps to ensure that the adult is emotionally and socially fit to work with young people. The procedure may also include a written application and a health screening (e.g., a tuberculosis test), as well as a criminal background check.

While all programs should sufficiently screen adults, deciding on who can be a mentor and who cannot is a highly subjective procedure. Before the selection process takes place, those adults perceived as being "successful" or worth emulating are usually preferred. I question the narrow scope of such decisions, particularly when considering the child who may only need someone to confide in. Does a youngster desiring an open ear actually require someone making $50,000 a year just to listen to him? Further, when we make an adult's social status a leading prerequisite for being a "good mentor," are we not discounting those other adults who, despite our social judgments, hold some measure of social and cultural significance for a youngster?

Although applying a stringent yardstick to measure who can be a mentor helps programs distinguish whether or not an adult is safe, trustworthy, and responsible, it can also restrict us from clearly seeing the talents and competencies an adult possesses and what this could mean to a youngster. At face value, we have seen those adults who perceptibly have no talents or gifts to contribute; we have hastily chalked them up as lazy, useless, dumb, dysfunctional, as dropouts, gang members, or ex-convicts; we have made no effort to see the value in these individuals or recognize the tangible contributions that they could make by working with young people.

If we can readjust our yardstick to include adults who seemingly have nothing to offer, yet are dependable, youth-centered, caring, respectful, and empathetic, we can tap a hidden supply of individuals who readily want to play a positive role in the lives of youth. We can no longer shortchange our children and our communities by not inviting the participation of these adults. Rather, we must make a genuine effort to see the residents of all neighborhoods, no matter how rich or poor, as potentially impacting mentors and reach out to them. Indeed, this is the reciprocal nature of mentoring: as adults embrace and support the lives of youth, they, in turn, can find a measure of acceptance, endearment, and contribution in the process.

In spite of the number of youth mentoring programs that exist and the assortment of curriculum that they have to offer, the basic intent of each should remain the same: to reach out and embrace young people with love and understanding, regardless of skin color, ethnicity, class, gender, ability, or belief system. Youth mentoring is a social responsibility, as well as a labor of love. It is about helping *all* youth understand who they are, assisting them in building a healthy self-concept, and supporting them in their dreams, visions, and goals.

Mentoring is not necessarily following a strict set of guidelines or procedures in any one particular environment. It is the kind of endeavor that seeks to know and engage young people in the multiple social spaces that they occupy. As mentors, teachers, and parents, we can always strive to know and understand the lives of young folks better—acknowledging their differences and similarities, offering them real-life experiences, listening to their ideas and supporting their dreams, celebrating their achievements and helping them correct their errors, loving and respecting them, balancing the scales for them, and offering them keys to doors that are often or otherwise locked.

Mentoring Young Men of Color communicates the practice of mentoring as curriculum in a broad sense. Distinct from the often prescriptive and narrow layout of academic goals and objectives, the viewpoints expressed here seek to address the often misunderstood lives of young males of color and the methods that we can use to assist them, in and outside of the school setting.

In the next chapter, I undertake a brief discussion of adolescent development as it plays out in the in-school experiences of males of color. In looking at their school lives, I also present three common obstacles that they face in this setting. I go on to present the concept of the *Act of Removal*. Essentially, it is a method of creating liberating and democratic learning environments where students have an active voice. Understanding how the *Act of Removal* functions in educational institutions can make all the difference in establishing successful SBM programs, as well as building positive teaching and learning environments. The ideas presented in chapter 2 mainly address mentoring within the school setting.

2

Embracing Young Males of Color in the School Domain

The road to freedom is paved with education.
It is the Blackest thing that you can do.

—Frederick Douglass

Adolescence marks a decisively pivotal time in human development. During these years, young people (ages 13–18) are experiencing multi-dimensional growth on various levels: intellectual, physical, social, moral, intrapersonal, and spiritual. This developmental stage finds adolescents engaged in both a conscious and unconscious search for an autonomous identity (i.e., a social role in life). It is the kind of search that is considerably influenced by peers and adults whose interactions and feedback assist adolescents in clarifying, as well as forming judgments about, the world around them. Here, the adolescent identity is partly constructed by sharing perspectives and personal experiences with others.

Outside of their social relationships, adolescents are also impacted by internal forces such as puberty, egocentrism, sexual orientation and confusion, insecurity, disillusionment, and depression. Within the matrix of these inner and outer dynamics, youth shape an image of themselves that can extend well into their adulthood. Specifically, for males of color, adolescence is burdened by such factors as hypermasculinity, racial awareness in a predominantly White society, negative

17

imagery tied to minority status, and social labeling and mistreatment—
all of which serve as high hurdles in understanding the Self. Consequently, the manifestation of these complexities can be seen in boys'
low academic achievement, delinquency, substance abuse, premature
sexual activity, alienation, and acts of aggression and violence toward
others.

Within the educational setting there exists a lived reality among
males of color that is widely foreign among teachers and school administrators. In the primary grades, schools are initially regarded by these
boys as safe and pleasant spaces for play, success, and fair gain. Yet, as
they progress into early adolescence they begin to view schools as being
no different than any other social institution that maligns and devalues
their culture and existence. Indeed, by the time these young men are
well into their teens they have already come to see schools as sites of
intolerance, oppression, and dehumanization. It is this perception that
pushes many of them to disconnect from classroom learning experiences, as well as disidentify with formal education on the whole.

Academic failure and disidentification for males of color is a consequence of three overarching factors. The first relates to present-day
classroom curriculum. As the adolescent male of color seeks out his
social role, he finds no clue of it in textbooks or classroom activities
that largely reflect Eurocentric frameworks and perspectives. From
social studies to the sciences, and from language arts to mathematics,
much of the curriculum that students of color are exposed to is short of
cultural representation and social relevancy. Teacher lesson plans that
coincide with required textbooks either minimize cultural aspects of
Latino and African American students or omit them altogether.

Students of color bring different histories and values into the classroom. As such, they must be presented with a curriculum that is rich
in cultural images and that helps them affirm and celebrate their educational experience. The added dimensions of social and cultural relevancy within a school curriculum can assist students of color in making
connections between what they are learning in school and its utility in
their out-of-school lives. Without seeing this vital correlation, students

of color will continue to resist the educative process, acting out in classrooms and wondering: "Where is my culture in this activity?" and "What does this lesson have to do with my life?"

With the above query in mind, teachers must strive to incorporate into their pedagogy the kind of curriculum that genuinely addresses student cultural values, beliefs, and norms. One significant resource to assist teachers in structuring lesson plans that highlight social and cultural concepts is the students themselves. By simply talking with each other, teachers and students can bring to the surface what attracts and excites and what bores and repels learners from learning.

Through open and honest dialogue, educators place themselves in the position of becoming more aware of the complex identities that each student possesses. With this newer knowledge, teachers not only learn how to reach students on a cognitive level but also how to connect with them on an affective one. Ideally, curriculum shifts from being Eurocentric to multicultural, from rigid to flexible, from mechanical to humanistic, and from isolating to embracing.

The second factor associated with academic failure and disidentification among males of color is the negative treatment that they encounter in schools and classrooms. If these boys walk, talk, or act in any manner contrary to school disciplinary codes, they are reprimanded without counsel, advocacy, or compassion. It is in this cold and unfeeling environment that boys begin to make out the unspoken agenda of schools—to silence and regulate their young lives. As school officials uphold callous, zero tolerance measures, they—unknowingly or not—foster much of the educational apathy and resistance that we are currently witnessing amid Latino and African American males.

When students of color are perceived as being "aggressive," "loud," or "out of control," on the surface we see it as a behavioral problem—something corrected through rules and regulation. But this typical response often stems from the fact that school faculty and staff do not have a firm understanding of students' physical development or cultural norms. As stated, adolescence is a period of tremendous physical growth. Young people are literally developing right in front of our eyes.

Because of the amount of growth occurring during this time, many students, particularly boys, find it extremely difficult to sit still, much less concentrate on a teacher's lesson. Young people desire movement. Yet, if they act on that impulse, they realize that they may be subjected to swift and harsh punishment. Invariably, at some point their desire will override their awareness of potential consequences, and the risk of moving or in some way expressing themselves will be taken.

Discipline problems often stem from how male student actions are perceived by teachers, usually female teachers. Boys, as compared to their female counterparts, are often stereotyped as being less thoughtful, less sensitive, less quiet, and less cooperative. When the constructions of race and class are added to gender, knowledge or ignorance of cultural norms plays a growing role in how we see and experience males of color.

There frequently exists among female teachers a kind of tension, confusion, or, sometimes, contempt for the social and cultural norms of males of color. Some White teachers, and even teachers of color from a higher socioeconomic status, tend to misinterpret or have little tolerance for the behaviors of Latino and African American students. Accordingly, they impose sanctions more regularly and more cruelly on these young people, leading to greater conflict and disidentification with their schooling.

This is not to say that female teachers, White or otherwise, cannot reliably teach nor have a profound effect on male students of color. Rather, it is to say that not knowing, understanding, and adequately addressing male student needs and behaviors generally results in their negative treatment. Not knowing their neighborhoods, what they face at home and in the streets, incredibly limits perception and understanding. With the lack of effort to be more sensitive and aware, teachers, both female and male, focus more on acquiescence and control.

When teachers fail to understand a student's ethnic experience or their acts of resistance to conformity, they then form negative perceptions of their students, seeing only audacity and disobedience. Associated with teacher negative attitudes and expectations is the student's internalization of these perceptions and their adaptation to them. Many students absorb negative teacher impressions, which can have adverse effects on their behavior, self-esteem, self-concept, and academic success.

In part, males of color suffer failure in schools and classrooms because the way they look, behave, speak, and learn is seen as divergent from what is deemed "normal." Boys then internalize these outward perceptions and perpetuate self-defeating behaviors both in and out of school. Sadly, their parents lose hope and wash their hands of them and teachers conveniently get rid of them through suspension, expulsion, and special education referrals.

In short, cultural perceptions guide the hand of disciplinary action. If we are adverse to a certain behavior, we often seek to control its occurrence through punishment and sanction. In the school setting, this translates into the controlling of student bodies through suspension and expulsion. The trouble with such measures is that they fail to take into account a student's cultural, emotional, or psychological outlook, which is most likely the source of the behavior. The major fault in school suspension and expulsion is that it merely removes the body from sight. It does not address the student's feelings, issues, or concerns. Thus, the problem, having never been dealt with appropriately, will only resurface with quite possibly greater impact and harsher restraint.

Like the structural disadvantages found within the larger society (discussed in the prologue), schools, unknowingly or not, construct barriers that discourage, demotivate, and disempower young males of color vis-à-vis curriculum and discipline. Just as these students are aware of the out-of-school barriers that exist, they are also cognizant of day-to-day in-school ones. The school building and virtually everything within it represents some form of barrier. Boys of color see barriers in their watered-down curriculum, their dead-end courses, and their biased achievement tests; they feel them in teachers' low expectations and the "discipline and punish" codes of their school; they wear them as drab, monochromatic school uniforms; and they hear them in classrooms where their cultural tongue remains undervalued and silenced.

One way or another, all students rebel against in-school barriers, particularly if they are sensitive to the effects. For males of color, rebellion can become routine in an environment where curriculum lacks cultural representations and where an excess of physical restrictions abound. Certainly, it is not difficult to understand their reactions to schooling given the conditions that these young men are subjected to on a daily basis. Yet despite the stark institutional realities that they face, there exists a third and final barrier that heightens academic failure and resistance among young males of color. It is an obstacle that they themselves construct and participate in to the detriment of their own personal development and success. In the following section, I offer a discussion on what is called the "Blame Game."

THE BLAME GAME: PERSONAL ACCOUNTABILITY UNACCOUNTED FOR

When discussing social and political inequities with adolescent males of color, the overall sentiment they share is that they are victims of prejudice and discrimination. In many instances they perceive teachers, administrators, and policemen as a combined enemy—a singular force whose objective is to silence their individual expression and prevent them from achieving their self-defined "American Dream." The more these students encounter authoritarian teachers, as well as policies and procedures that regulate their existence, the more schools become part and parcel to a discriminatory experience. Schools begin to reflect the larger society, and these young men come to see both settings as cold, unwelcoming, and biased.

So how do males of color react to institutional racism? How do they deal with their victimization? In response to many of the in-school injustices that they face, these students tend to use oppositional methods that ironically mirror their own oppression. For example, when they suffer verbal discipline from school staff, males will retort with their own curse words and threats; when they feel overlooked by teachers, they will ignore classroom lessons or leave work uncompleted; when they feel unwanted or alienated by the school at large, they will in turn disconnect, disengage, and ultimately drop out.

In their attempt to challenge the in-school barriers that stifle their identity and ways of being, males of color simultaneously construct another obstacle that further impedes their social and academic success. It is an obstacle that faults teachers and other institutional agents for students' lack of achievement, while never once recognizing how students themselves are complicit in their own personal and collective failures. This is called the "Blame Game"—it is a long, drawn-out contest of finger-pointing.

As a social phenomenon, the Blame Game is nothing new. Our society has engaged in it for some time. The objective of the game is to remove oneself from all personal accountability. Whatever failures or setbacks one encounters, the burden must be shifted away from the individual and placed onto someone else. Everyone has played this game. We have all pointed fingers. Perhaps we have pointed at politicians and their policy decisions or toward an educator and his or her approach to teaching or at a parent and his or her method of child rearing and supervision. In whatever direction we have pointed our fingers, rarely have we included ourselves in that scope.

Undeniably, we have all joined in on the Blame Game. Yet while we play, we inadvertently teach young people this diversionary tactic. We show them that it is much easier to believe that someone else is responsible for their losses without demonstrating to them how to overcome their defeats. They then take our lessons into schools and reproduce them. They come to realize that if they do not do well in school, then it is obvious who must be to blame—the teacher. Indeed, this is the main problem with the Blame Game. It does not force us to look critically at ourselves. It does not ask us to make personal changes within our lives or to work collectively toward social reform. Instead, we condemn others for our individual mistakes as well as those errors that occur on a larger social scale.

As a response to their everyday oppressive circumstances, young males of color are angry. In many respects, we have entitled them to feel this way. We have given them license to abhor society and themselves because we have not provided them with the necessary tools to move beyond the Blame Game. These males require our assistance in redirecting their power, confronting their pain, transcending their rage, and organizing themselves to create a better, more constructive way of being. This is called personal agency; it runs contrary to blame. As opposed to performing random acts of self-destruction, these young men should be supported in building a healthy mind, body, and spirit. Further, by presenting them with alternative modes of teaching and learning, they can cease blaming another for their lack of academic achievement and take control of their own educational destiny.

The next section looks at the role that mentors and teachers must first be willing to play in order to foster personal agency within males of color. It involves shifting from the traditional authoritarian directives that have become common in our educative practices. I informally call this shift the *Act of Removal*. Inspired by the works of John Dewey and Paulo Freire, it is an educational tool that can be used to assist students and educators in overcoming the powerlessness that the Blame Game embodies. While schools have historically and presently been sites of assimilation and control, the Act of Removal holds the potential for turning learning environments into democratically safe spaces of academic freedom and emotional release.

THE ACT OF REMOVAL
It is ironic that in American society we advance democratic ideals, while in our schools and classrooms we promote dictatorships. In over 150 years of institutional education, teachers still situate themselves as the all-knowing and all-powerful figure in the classroom. From years of working in public schools, as both a teacher and a mentor, I am well aware of the power that teachers possess as the authority figure. While we can be attentive, caring, sensitive, and loving practitioners, we can also be strict, judgmental, cruel, and controlling autocrats.

While it is sometimes easy for us to confuse authority with omnipotence, we must try to break away from the "my way or the highway" mentality that is pervasive in teaching and instruction. Instead, we must make the attempt to subordinate ourselves and come to see schools and classrooms as ethical sites, where students can be the creators of their own learning experience and teachers can be the facilitators of that knowledge. This is the Act of Removal. It is a process whereby classrooms become less dominated by adult authority and more youth-centered and focused. The objective is to construct learning environments that foster youth empowerment, free expression, self-discipline, and self-respect. With these notions in the forefront of our educative practices, student resistance to classroom learning can be minimized.

In carrying out the Act of Removal, teachers must first be conscious of how the misuse of their authoritarian power can negatively impact classroom learning and student life. Once teachers are aware of this, the Act of Removal asks them to take a risk—that is, to share this power with student participants. In short, learning becomes a partnership. This type of approach has been mirrored in the use of teacher–student contracts, where attendance policies, in-class activities, assessments, and other conventional practices are agreed upon jointly. For example, teachers may present various topics within a specific discipline, but dialogue with students about multiple ways of exploring it. As opposed to laying out a forced lesson plan or set of classroom rules, students and teachers approach everything as a collaborative endeavor. All voices are heard and validated in decision-making processes.

In spite of the power sharing that occurs during the Act of Removal, it is still essential for teachers to remain the classroom authority figure for it is the teacher who maintains a consistently safe and organized learning environment. Hence, subordinating oneself should be done inasmuch as is reasonable for producing and sustaining a secure classroom setting. This means instinctually and experientially knowing how much power to share with students based on their reaction to, and responsibility of, being a power holder and sharer. Without question, teachers must take baby steps as they employ the Act.

In some instances, the Act of Removal can be a cultural shock for teachers and students, particularly in schools where class culture and student life are so incredibly rigid and defined. In my own teaching practices, young folks have responded to the Act of Removal in three general ways: (1) they do not see the Act as an opportunity to express critical thought and voice, and thus squander it by continually looking to me as the absolute authority figure; (2) they abuse their power and misuse the opportunity for constructive voice and action by disrespecting other students and myself; or (3) at some point they come to recognize the power being shared with them and use it as an asset to enhance their overall schooling experience.

Of course, the above reactions are contingent upon each student's disposition. For example, some years ago I taught a seventh-grade class. As a social studies activity, I asked students to collectively develop a list of problematic school-related issues. Their rather extensive listing included the following: school uniforms, cafeteria food, limited field trips, and inadequate school space. They were then asked if they wanted to inform the school's administration and Parent-Teachers Association of these concerns. All students were in agreement. With that in mind, they had the option of remaining anonymous—a majority did not.

Next, they were to think of various ways to express themselves. At this point, a small portion of student involvement declined. Although a large part of the class took on leadership roles in developing videos, audio recordings, and petitions, a minority abandoned their projects altogether, opting to disrespect their peers by engaging in name-calling and clowning around during audio and video recordings. In this instance, my role as the authority figure found me maintaining a safe space by talking one-on-one with those students who were disruptive. I either asked them to think of other ways to express their issues or to engage in a completely separate activity of their choice. They were split in the decision.

Despite varying student responses to the Act of Removal, bringing genuine democracy into classrooms affords young people the chance to speak their voice (even in their own vernacular); make choices based on their own perspective, culture, and experience; and challenge authority (which includes dominant ideologies) without fear of being reprimanded. As for teachers, theoretically they become more flexible and open to various student ideas. With these outcomes in mind, schools and classrooms can ideally become more welcoming, less restrictive, and less suffocating environments for all participants.

The Act of Removal helps educators become less dictatorial in their teaching role and more like partners in the learning experience. When teachers remove themselves from the authoritarian role that their position assumes, students can then learn to become stakeholders in their own education. As stakeholders, students learn to be more proactive in their learning and less reactive (i.e., the Blame Game). As for the educational setting, it becomes more personal and less callous. Students and teachers come to see each other as fully human, presenting one another with the opportunity to develop meaningful and long-lasting relationships.

Just as the Act of Removal asks teachers to create a leveled playing field within the learning environment, the same goes for school-based mentors. When mentoring in the classroom, it is important for mentors to take a step back every now and then, close their mouths, and open their ears to the range of thoughts and feelings being expressed by their mentees. Often mentors, like teachers, feel the need to stand in front of classrooms and preach to students about the dos and don'ts of life—a sort of one-way conversation where students wind up tuning out and turning off.

As opposed to sermonizing to young folks, we need to place their needs, their issues, and their voices at the center of mentoring sessions. We must remember that embracing environments cannot be created through one-way conversations. School-based mentoring must meet young people where they are emotionally and psychologically by providing them with a time and a space to articulate their lives, as well as the opportunity to release any repressed emotions. After listening to what they have to say, mentors may then step in and assist mentees in navigating their expressed issues. Mentoring of this nature is far more attractive to young people than that which lectures, moralizes, or attempts to "fix" them.

Helping students disclose their inner thoughts and emotions may require that mentors do the same. Young people need to know that the road to adulthood is difficult for everyone, and that it does not necessarily lead to perfection. Indeed, the mentor is very much human and subject to error. Revealing oneself can be a risk—the kind of risk that the Act of Removal entails. In the context of mentoring and teaching, it means showing our humanity—warts and all.

One way to make our humanity known is by telling students some of our own personal stories. This includes our failures, as well as our accomplishments. Personal stories hold the potential for connecting with students on deeper levels. As we open up and disclose ourselves to them, they are more easily able to relate to us and see that we share many of the same traits and qualities as they do. The information that we provide might even serve as a life lesson for them to learn from.

Some of the personal stories that I have shared with my own mentees have ranged from run-ins with the police as a teenager to my near dropout from high school and from my graduation from college to the present struggles that I face as an adult. By talking about my everyday triumphs and defeats, some of my mentees are able to see themselves in me and connect on a more humanistic level. From this, we are able to further extend our lines of communication and continue to build meaningful relationships based on honesty, trust, and mutual respect.

The Act of Removal gives mentors and educators the chance to transform hierarchical classrooms and relationships into equitable learning communities, where youth and adults are positioned laterally. This form of humanism is reliant upon all participants recognizing and accepting each other's respective roles, identities, and voices. In the next chapter, I address more specifically the space that young males of color need to have in order to excel in the school environment. This space not only incorporates the Act of Removal but also other components and classroom techniques that serve to enrich the schooling experience for young males of color.

3

Constructing a Space for Boys

Tell me and I'll forget; show me and I may remember; involve me and I'll understand.

—Chinese proverb

THE ROLE OF SCHOOL-BASED MENTORS

As touched on in the previous chapter, formal schooling for males of color can be a horribly oppressive experience. When they are treated in ways that either discount or invalidate who they are as individuals and as a social group, the air in educational settings can be extremely suffocating. Indeed, much of what is taught and practiced in schools is perceived by these males as both counterintuitive and counterproductive. If a school's culture unwittingly perpetuates this grievous experience, then SBM programs, geared toward uplifting males of color, must not only be mindful of this reality but also willing to construct an in-school space that genuinely functions to offset this aspect of student life.

In some cases, a space for boys is purely just that—an all-male mentee and mentor setting. By no means does this insinuate that female mentors are incapable of contributing to male forums. Quite the contrary, women have much to say that can inform males of the conscious and unconscious aspects of masculinity and how it impacts gender relationships. Nevertheless, girls and boys often need separate spaces away from their gender counterparts in order to have free expression and prevent intimidation. Once their personal views are placed on the table, then it is more than conceivable for girl and boy groups to combine their respective forums and discuss their issues collectively. In the meantime, let us look at ways of building a space strictly for boys.

Constructing a mentoring space for young males of color does not necessarily mean hanging Che Guevara and Malcolm X posters around the room or playing the latest hip hop music. While this can strike a chord with the cultural side of students, we are more concerned with creating an environment that affords young men of color a chance to breathe—the kind of space that runs contrary to the stifling air of the everyday classroom, a space that is relatively free from rigid classroom rules, low teacher expectations, deculturalized curriculum, and the overuse of power. A space where boys are free to move around and assemble, where they can express who they are without being labeled, where they can be real without posing for their female counterparts, where they can strive to understand themselves in the context of the world around them, and where they can inhale and then release.

The prime component that adult mentors must address in constructing a space for boys is the need for a safe environment. Safety constitutes physical, mental, and emotional domains and must be established for all participants. Safe spaces must be free from psychological and physical violence, judgment, ridicule, and disrespect, especially if we desire for males to open up and share personal feelings and information. Safe spaces include, as much as possible, care, comfort, free expression, empathy, concern, mutual respect, love, understanding, attentive ears, and open minds. Being that young people thrive in stable environments, there must be a consistency in all of these things.

Part of creating a safe mentoring space, for the sake of having young males open up, is showing them that you, as the adult male, are comfortable in sharing your own experiences. By doing so we send the message that it is safe for boys to be themselves in this space. If we want to see and hear young men express their true selves without posturing, then it is critical that we reveal our true selves, as adult males, without posturing. In order to get boys to feel safe and to reveal emotion, school-based mentors must also open up and show them that expressing emotions and being a man are not mutually exclusive acts.

At very young ages, males of color are taught that being a "man" means holding back emotions, sucking in the tears, but externalizing aggression. School-based mentors concerned with the inner nature of Latino and African American boys must provide them with an appropriately open space to release and communicate their feelings. By creating cathartic environments for males of color to vent, we help alleviate some of the tension and anxiety that they encounter on a daily basis and also repress on an unconscious level. Thus, in the space that we are sharing with boys, group discussions should function as a productive means for minimizing their stress, whether hidden, restrained, or unrecognized.

An illustration of the open and safe space that we are building for young males of color comes from a personal experience. In a school-based mentoring session with a group of middle-school boys, one of the program units focused on domestic violence. I showed a video on spousal abuse to prepare the boys for a guest speaker who was scheduled to come in the following week. In the video, four women discussed their stories about the victimization they suffered at the hands of their husbands. As the women discussed their exploitation in full detail, some of the boys shook their heads in disgust and disbelief. When the video ended, I opened the floor to dialogue.

I asked the boys about their view on each woman's tale of abuse. They looked around the room as if waiting for someone to speak first, so I decided to initiate the conversation. I told them my personal account of growing up and witnessing the verbal and emotional abuse that my mother faced from my stepfather. I disclosed to them the rage and powerlessness that I felt seeing this as a child and the extreme violent thoughts that I entertained.

After I finished, a student chimed in sharing a similarly dramatic story about the physical abuse that his mother endures from her boyfriend, and how the experience fuels his sadness and anger. After him, another young man revealed the fear that he faces each morning on his way to school when local gangs try to recruit him through threat and intimidation. One by one, each boy stood up and spoke matter-of-factly about the various forms of violence in their lives and the stress that they feel as a result.

From this example, we can see that honest and safe mentoring spaces help boys articulate emotions that are often left muted or pent up. In order for mentors to create and build upon this kind of space, they must be prepared to contribute to group discussions in sincere and heartfelt ways. As boys come to feel comfortable and safe with you and the environment, they open up in ways that the regular classroom does not allow and cannot generate. In this newer, more secure space, boys can share their feelings, form their own understandings around personal issues, and see that they are not alone in their private situations.

It is through authentic dialogue that we truly come to know who our young people are, placing mentors in positions to provide them with wisdom, knowledge, and a clearer understanding of the world that they are living in. Presenting them with the time and the opportunity to speak vastly differs from the regular classroom where "time on task" is the major focus and where what is taught is usually expressed through the singular lens of a text or the imperious voice of a teacher. School-based mentors must strive to create a more relaxed air—one that includes multiple voices and perspectives.

Learning communities that allow males of color to positively express themselves give these young people an opportunity to breathe. As opposed to governing their minds through prescribed curriculum and regulating their bodies through harsh discipline codes, we must offer them a chance to interject their own thoughts and viewpoints into the schooling experience—*their* schooling experience. It is their expression that informs us of their individual needs, temperament, personality, and identity. From this, we can learn how to genuinely connect with them and support whatever aspirations they hold.

Constructing a space for males of color demands that their ideas be at the center of program curriculum and practices. If we ignore or silence them—and we have observed that outcome time and time again—they disengage or rebel. Even though our space must have rules to ensure protection for all participants, it is not about control. Rather, it is about providing them with a time and a place to be understood as children and teenagers; to be free, criticial thinkers; to express their inner thoughts; and to be embraced as males of color.

THE ROLE OF SBM CURRICULUM

The notion of encouraging students to inquire and analytically think about their world, as well as proffering alternative avenues in their decision-making processes, differs immensely from the unilateral, direct-instructional way of teaching that is typical in our educational institutions. As opposed to filling student minds with a disjointed reality devoid of any real significance, mentors and mentees must discuss and discover their individual perceptions and identities, as well as ways of personally evolving and transforming their lives for the present and future.

The school-based mentoring curriculum ought to be socially and culturally relevant for males of color. It must inform them of what is happening in the world around them, draw connections from those events to their life, and enlighten them as to the various choices that they can make and the consequences of those decisions. The idea of such a curriculum is also about helping males alter or avoid stressful conflicts as they encounter them on a personal and everyday basis.

We are well aware of those young men who deal with their stress in destructive ways given that constructive avenues to express themselves have been closed off or made otherwise inaccessible. These young men commit deviant acts in small spaces (e.g., the classroom, the neighborhood block) to make their personal power seem bigger. Their rebellious acts are outward expressions of their need to have power over something and be recognized and understood. Hence, SBM curriculum for males of color must touch and ignite the creative side within them—the side that seeks to build and not to destroy, to release and not to suppress, to give and not to withhold. The following are a few possibilities to include in the design and implementation of SBM and/or classroom curriculum.

Arts-Based Activities

One way that mentors can tap into the affective side of boys, bringing their emotions to the surface and into a discussion, is through the use of arts-based activities. Youth of all ages are drawn to the arts. They empower and encourage young people to come up with ideas that resonate within their own worlds, putting them in control of their own understanding and motivating them to learn, discover, imagine, and achieve. Once students are empowered to think and act on their own, they can take control over their own learning and life. Ideally, this promotes personal agency, self-discipline, self-respect, and self-defined expectations.

Arts-based activities also provide self-activation, where students can speak their own language and not worry about adult perfection. Mediums of expression like poetry, spoken word, hip hop, and sketch artistry serve as vehicles for youth to convey their complex identities and emotions. Through such artistic forms, boys are able to communicate their issues, name their social anxieties, and shape their experiences in ways that are inhibited by conventional speech.

One arts-based project that a group of students and I initiated was called *Real Voices*. This SBM endeavor was a showcase of creative youth expressions where boys were able to openly verbalize about and reflect on the day-to-day highs and lows of school and home life. Using mainly poetry and hip hop, they discussed how they learned to deal with those issues that impacted their life: teenage fatherhood, hostile neighborhoods, gun violence, gang warfare, domestic violence, substance abuse, and peer pressure.

The Real Voices project proved to be an empowering experience for its participants. While they were engaged in a sixteen-week process of writing, editing, expressing their voices, and recording, a shift in their attitude toward school was revealed—attendance increased, behavioral problems declined, and their grades improved. Indeed, the boys became more committed to learning as they transformed project initiatives into their own creation. Moreover, doing so afforded them the chance to speak their own dialect without worrying about "official" arrangements of language.

The frankness of their cultural tongue on this project, as well as in our mentoring sessions, further created a space dissimilar from the regular classroom. While it is the job of teachers to help students master Standard English, often that is done at the cost of abandoning one's way of speaking altogether. This "cultural tongue," as it were, symbolizes the most powerful force of human identity. It represents both culture and language. Urging young men of color to give it up in many ways forces them to sacrifice an enormous aspect of who they are. The reality is that students possess their own languages, both informal and official. Not to embrace the former, in some degree, can promote student silencing, as well as resistance.

When we invite Latino and African American males to bring their culture and language into the SBM setting, we reduce the conflict that exists between these students and the larger school culture by validating their identity. Unlike the everyday classroom, students are not asked to solely use Standard English. In SBM settings, they can freely intersperse words such as "dope" (meaning something superb) or "whacked" (meaning something stupid or boring) with the "King's English." It is critical that boys be allowed to use their vernacular and not feel restricted by doing so.

For the most part, young people know the difference between their informal tongue and the official one. What they need assistance in understanding is that they do not have to relinquish one for the sake of the other. They can learn to master Standard English for the benefit of excelling in academics and in the job world, while retaining their individual tongue for the purpose of being able to communicate with members of their immediate culture and avoiding the "sellout" label. Without a doubt, we must teach youth of color when and where it is appropriate to switch their language. This leads to a brief, but critical, point on this subject.

On the Real Voices project, I felt that it was inappropriate for boys to use curse words (e.g., "shit" or "damn") to accentuate their feelings or thoughts on a particular issue. While the everyday rap songs they listen to liberally use such language, the CD that we were creating was to be distributed and played among teachers, parents, peers, and younger children. In this case, the boys fully understood that using profanity would be unsuitable. They also came to understand that creating a safe and respectful mentoring environment for everyone meant staying away from homosexual and racially offensive slurs such as "bitch," "faggot," and even "nigger." In later sections of this chapter, I discuss ways of having a critical dialogue with boys surrounding gender stereotypes and the derogatory language attached to it.

Besides arts-based activities, how else can school-based mentors build open and constructive environments? What other forms of curriculum can be used to assist boys in disclosing their emotions, their problems, and even their views on the larger society? In line with arts-based activities, boys ought to be engaged in something that is culturally meaningful and socially relevant, something that is arousing and informative, and something that takes them out of the passive spectator role and places them in a position where they can freely interpret and respond to curriculum as it fits within the context of their own life, and in the lives of significant others.

Reflective Writing

While arts-based activities assist in exploring boys' creative dimensions, they can occasionally fall short in getting at the root of who they are beyond male posturing. Here, I am specifically referring to the artistic expression of hip hop. Although rap lyrics cleverly narrate lived reality, males sometimes take on another persona through hip hop, usually replicating and glorifying the false images of male bravado that they see in biased media and popular music. Mentors must be aware of these skewed representations and how they help to shape young male perceptions and identities and must urge boys to be more than just passive consumers of them. Accordingly, SBM curriculum must incorporate a critical perspective—one that delves deeper into the individual and shared perspectives of males of color.

An example of such curriculum comes out of one of my mentoring sessions with a group of high-school boys. I brought in a recent newspaper article about a twelve-year-old boy, Orlando Patterson, who had been shot and killed playing outside his home in the West Englewood community of Chicago. For me, stories about youth violence can be startling and distressing. Yet, I wondered how these young males responded to daily violence in their own lives, whether on television, in newspapers, in music, in school, and possibly in their homes. I was curious to know not only what they felt and thought about it but also how they came to terms with it.

I familiarized the students with the newspaper story and passed out copies of it. I also brought in an audio tape of two songs related to some of the adversities that urban youth face. The first song was R. Kelly's "Gotham City" and the second was Mista's "Blackberry Molasses." As the music played, I asked the boys to think about the article and write down their responses to it. As they wrote, R. Kelly soulfully crooned in the background about ghetto life—of no money and no friends, of no food and no clothing—and the need for a change.

As the second song faded, students still continued to write. When all pens were down, I asked if there was anyone who wanted to read his response aloud. In the little time that was left in our session, several of the boys shared their thoughts and personal experiences related to violence. They spoke about the loss of friends and family members to gang violence; they expressed the anger and uncertainty surrounding their own lives; they questioned the reasons for Orlando Patterson's murder; and they wondered why it had to happen. One student was even driven to tears while reading his response.

Seeing and hearing all their different reactions, I found the meeting to be overtly cathartic. Many of the hostile environments and circumstances that evidently pervaded these boys' lives needed to be vented. The boys had a lot to say about physical violence and the fatal end that it can sometimes lead to. Although our arts-based activities were fun and productive, they did not evoke the same kind of emotion and personal exchange as this writing activity. Putting their immediate thoughts on paper, without rhyme or verse, proved to be a positive outlet for expression. It was the kind of action that provided a space and time for these boys to process thought and emotion—an act that some males of color avoid or ignore, which unfortunately leaves them less in touch with themselves and less informed about ways of bettering their situation. In our next group session, we revisited their writings and discussed various hostile elements of life and constructive ways for handling them.

Conflict Resolution

Another viable option for encouraging males of color to reflect on and talk about their lives is through the use of conflict resolution skits. As a peer group activity, conflict resolution supports and enables students to play an intricate role in their self-development by having them collectively problematize, articulate, understand, and possibly transform their shared world in both in and out of school locations. Conflict resolution is a vital curriculum component in school-based mentoring as it puts students in real-life situations and asks them to develop rational choices to conflict. The purpose is to acquaint students with choices that they can reasonably consider in addition to the ones that they are already used to.

Boys tend to resolve conflict based on how their immediate surrounding environment functions and what it dictates. Some boys are taught that if someone pushes you, then you have to push back. While this is common, these decisions can sometimes lead to a fatal end. Of course, it depends on who is doing the pushing and who is pushed. The purpose of conflict resolution is to urge boys to think beyond the moment and to see that responding to situations with violence (verbal, physical, or psychological) is not always the answer. By offering them multiple options to everyday conflict, boys become better equipped in knowing how to handle hostile situations without jeopardizing their own well-being and future.

As mentors, it is important that the choices and solutions we offer be practical and realistic to the lives of mentees. When using peer groups, mentors should talk with boys about their options but not suppress any one particular way of thinking or rule of thumb in the way that they should manage their lives. It is not about telling boys what to do or how to be. Rather, it is opening up a dialogue with them, discussing choices to solving a dilemma, alerting them to the consequences of those choices, asking them what they think about those decisions, and trusting them to pick the least destructive and harmful outcome.

In one of our mentoring sessions, another colleague and I placed thirty middle-school boys into six groups of five. We informed them that in handling conflicting situations they have three basic alternatives to choose from: accepting it, altering it, or avoiding it. We gave each group a hypothetical situation and asked them to develop skits based on these three alternatives. Afterward, they would perform their skits in front of their classmates.

The first group performed a sketch in which a teacher was reprimanding a student for talking in class. In their presentation, the boys portrayed the teacher as infuriated and unwilling to listen to the student. Each boy alternated between playing the teacher while the other acted out one of the three choices that they could make in the confrontation. In their first example, they showed a student accepting the situation by not talking back to the teacher and suffering under his angry words. The conclusion was that the student was suspended.

In the second skit, a student avoided the conflict altogether by not talking in the classroom. The third option showed the student altering the situation by first listening to what the teacher had to say and then respectfully explaining his reason for talking in class. Although the boys felt that the teacher would be unwilling to listen, they believed that by showing respect they might elude suspension, as well as further admonishment. The boys then added a fourth skit which showed the student not talking back to the teacher, but then later telling a mentor about the situation. One of the boys portrayed a mentor calmly talking to the teacher about the student, helping the boy get out of trouble.

Despite their range in age (10–14), we found that this activity was engaging for boys, as they were able to express themselves through the physical activity of acting, cooperation with peers, and the conveyance of personal issues and concerns. The conflict resolution activity also helped to teach the skill of thinking beyond the moment, of seeing other ways of being. It encouraged our boys to question their everyday ways of thinking and reacting by considering alternative ways of handling life situations.

Other than discussions surrounding in-school experiences, conflict resolution can address the following questions: what happens if we choose not to extend our education past high school; if we give in to peer pressure and engage in alcohol and drug use; if we have unprotected sex; if we maintain prejudiced notions of other cultures; if we never see the equality in gender; if we never come to know and discipline ourselves? In these discussions, there is no all-inclusive correct response. Rather, individuals have to decide which decisions are best for them in the context of their own lives and how their decisions can and will affect others.

Young males of color, as all youth, need to be involved in defining and shaping their world, whether it is in the classroom, the neighborhood, or the larger society. As mentors, we must provide them with a genuine sense of proactiveness, as opposed to the helplessness that can easily engulf their lives. Rather than being blindfolded contestants in the Blame Game, they can make wide-awake choices in working together with us to develop safe and realistic strategies for dealing with conflict.

Socially and Culturally Relevant Discussion Topics

In my own SBM program, I design and implement a curriculum that functions to inform and awaken boys to the external world around them. Topics are made socially and culturally relevant by demonstrating how they can potentially impact student life, despite the seemingly physical, social, and cultural distance between them.

For example, a tragic school incident such as the one in Columbine,

Colorado, is not just some distant, White, suburban issue. It represents an underbelly of violence that pervades even urban schools. On the subject of the criminal justice system, we have focused on juvenile jails and the ever-increasing restrictive laws against youth. Although the dreadful construction of youth jails and the unjust revisions of legal statutes are heavily occurring in states like Florida and California, the boys and I talk about how the expansion of these sorts of laws will one day infringe upon their own rights in their own state.

Mentoring sessions have found us examining racist stereotypes in popular culture, discussing how news stories and crime statistics inaccurately represent males of color, how these representations play on our self-concepts, and what we as males of color can do about it. By providing these young men with an understanding of how media images, violence, power, and racism work in their society, they come to see how these dynamics affect their personal decisions and life choices.

In one particular week of program meetings with high schoolers, I introduced a discussion on gender stereotypes. At the outset, I defined gender as a social construction that implied multiple differences between the categories of feminine and masculine. Group members were then given a diagram of three boxes. I explained that the larger center box represented ways in which we are meant to exist and feel as men. The pressure and abuse that we receive to keep us inside this box produce a range of emotions, which were listed in the center: anger, sadness, isolation, acceptance, and curiosity. Ironically, it is also within this box that we develop a sense of control, connection, and love with other males. If we deviate from this, then we are subjected to the verbal and physical abuses noted in the smaller left and right boxes, littered with words like "sissy," "punk," "bitch," and "fag."

I asked the boys if it was possible to exist outside the center box without suffering physical, verbal, and emotional abuse. Many of them said that it was not. They gave examples of peers who were outside the box and how they were teased or beaten up because of their individuality. I then asked the boys to think about the last time they were called a punk, a sissy, or a bitch because they did not live up to the social expectation of what it means to be male. Some of the boys revealed that such words were used daily and casually; others commented that they did not care what others said about them; some admitted that name-calling often lead to fights; some felt that it was okay to be inside the box, while others professed that it was not.

In this session, it was my hope that these young men would awaken and see the "boxes" of their lives that had already shaped and encapsulated them. I wanted to expose them to alternative ways of thinking, being, and acting as males of color. They needed to be shown choices apart from the ones they made on a daily basis. Although it is the hope that after having such a dialogue students will walk away with a clearer understanding, this is, of course, not always the case. Yet, exposing them to alternative ways of thinking and being presents an opportunity for boys to explore a different, more in-depth, perception, one that they might not be used to seeing.

Discussions revolving around issues of race, class, and gender ought not be designed to adjust the thinking of mentees to the thinking of mentors. Classroom curricula promote enough of this. In contrast, the purpose of such dialogue is to expose young people to concepts and perspectives that are both similar and different to that of their own. Mentors are merely presenting the multiple doors that exist, yet it is mentees who make the choice of crossing the threshold. Through this type of mentoring forum, boys are looking at their lives more critically, with the possibility of transforming themselves by means of a newly informed perspective. With multiple lenses to look through and knowledge of multiple avenues to take, our young males of color can begin to be less destructive and more constructive, less hopeless and more hopeful, less passive and more aggressive in making productive changes in their lives and in their communities. Indeed, knowledge is power.

Brotherhood

Socially and culturally relevant curricula afford young males an opportunity to communicate personal experiences with peers. As boys share and deconstruct their lived realities, kinships are formed. This sort of connection is either underdeveloped in classrooms or missing altogether. Having an open and accommodating place to discuss issues gives rise to feelings of camaraderie. Such feelings can offer strength and focus to students who are struggling socially and academically. Where before some have felt disconnected or alienated by their schooling experience, they are now participating in a kind of fellowship that socially connects them with their education. The curriculum that we engage our mentees in is more than just a series of objectives and outcomes. We are developing a human connection through a relevant and engaging curriculum that gives rise to identifying and sharing common personal experiences and goals—in short, a brotherhood.

The feeling of brotherhood in an all-male SBM forum is not a forced sentiment. One cannot expect a program to become a "brotherhood" or a "family" simply because these words are used in a program's title. What makes group mentoring transform into a brotherhood or family is that it provides young males with a safe forum that is based on trust and intimacy—something that is acquired over time. Once boys experience this level of intimacy, they often find ways to maintain closeness with peers, as well as with significant others in their life. For some males, this begins with brotherhood but can carry over into building healthy relationships with women, families, and communities.

One of my SBM experiences serves as an illustration of how SBM programs can create natural spaces where brotherhood is fostered. Mentoring a group of high-school seniors, I brought in a videotape that documented a newly constructed youth jail in California. After setting up the TV and VCR, the boys walked in with a look of utter exhaustion. I asked them what the problem was. Their response was that their teachers were increasing their workload as a way to push them academically. Moving the TV and VCR out of the way, I asked them to talk more about it.

The boys spoke rather candidly about the unachievable academic expectations that were placed upon them by the school staff. Apparently, a few of their teachers were conducting lessons at an extremely fast pace. Before students had time to digest one concept, their teachers were already onto the next one. They also went on to criticize their school's mission statement. As they were expected to follow it to the letter, they did not appreciate the school staff forcing these ideals upon them.

The boys also felt that the "egalitarian" principles cited in the school's mission statement did not correspond with the way many of them were treated in classrooms and in the school as a whole. When they asked for assistance on a particular activity, teachers ignored them, told them to ask another student, or accused them of disrupting the class. Further, many of their conflicts in the classroom were not handled fairly or diplomatically. According to these students, resolutions were often reached by the teacher through their removal from the classroom, after-school detention, out-of-school suspension, or parent–teacher conferences.

In our sixty minutes together, the boys and I talked about ways of changing this situation. One student brought up the idea of rebelling against the administration with a nonviolent protest. I replied that protest was one way to handle the problem and I would help them with it, but I urged them to think about other alternatives in handling their issues. We came up with other options like helping each other with class work and coming to me if they had any problems with a particular teacher. As for coping with the school's mission statement, the boys decided to follow it, while at the same time ignoring it. They felt that since they only had one year left, they would adhere to the rules until they successfully graduated from the school. At the end of our talk, the boys acknowledged that they felt much better. They were able to release their aggression and hostility by talking with one another. They called the session "group therapy."

Discussions, like the one above, help boys to critically look at their situation and respond to it constructively. By posing options to them, boys are able to pick and choose alternatives that they might not know exist or perceive as viable. Group discussions on this level expand student perceptions of the world and develop new ways of relating and interacting within it. Out of this dialogical practice comes the notion of brotherhood. Through collective examination of their world and realizing that they have the ability to organize and to make change, boys develop a strong sense of camaraderie and agency.

So what happens to those boys who desire adult guidance but do not want to be involved with group mentoring? Perhaps they do not get along with a specific classmate or their creative interests are not addressed by the program. Mentors can meet the needs of these students by continually offering them an invitation to program meetings, as well as encouragement toward the development of their own projects. In cases where these students choose not to be a part of the program at all, mentors should still offer them advocacy regardless of their disassociation. Also, SBM curriculum can assist alienated students in warming up to their peers by promoting group problem-solving projects or report-back research. Such activities engender peer communication and teamwork relationships that might not otherwise exist in the regular school curriculum. As this occurs, students who were once alienated can begin to see the value of social networking between cliques, as well as the value of their own individual personality and contribution.

4

Extending beyond a Space for Boys

If kids come to us from strong, healthy functioning families, it makes our job easier. If they do not come from strong, functioning families, it makes our job more important.

—Barbara Colorose

In chapter 3, we looked at various forms of curricular activities proven to create an openly cathartic and embracing space for young males of color. In one sense, the use of these curricular methods helps SBM programs to build a collection of artifacts, such as essays, poems, and drawings, which reflect the lives of mentees. In another sense, the curriculum serves to foster a genuine feeling of belongingness and brotherhood among its members. Yet, in a third sense, we can also observe what is achievable past the conveyance of this subject matter to extend beyond the four walls of the classroom.

ARTS-BASED CURRICULUM REVISITED

As discussed in the previous chapter, the overarching idea behind arts-based projects is to provide males of color with various mediums to express themselves. To engage them in these projects, it is important to offer a chance to elect what projects they want to do and how they want to pursue them. Whether it is an audio CD, a collage of student photos, a book of personal writings, or a video diary, the projects have to be

significant to participants, thus producing an engaged student environment.

Turning student engagement into empowerment often means taking
boys and their work outside of school. All the issues and ideas that they
have expressed through their art can be conveyed by them to members
in the broader community. No longer do they these young men have
to feel as if their voice is provincialized to their immediate surroundings. No longer do they have to live with the outlook that their needs
and concerns are inconsequential and unchangeable. When mentors
provide boys with a public space to vent their thoughts and emotions
to others, we implicitly teach them that a large part of the educative
experience can be directly translated and exercised within the larger
society. Furthermore, we show them the real world and the various
public spaces that they have access to. These critical life lessons teach
males of color that there are constructive approaches for articulating
their issues and making social changes, however large or small, without
jeopardizing their lives and futures.

An example of a public space that can provide boys with the opportunity to communicate their lives is a professional conference. In a
room filled with about forty educators and school administrators, a
handful of program mentees presented the reflective writings on the
tragedy of the twelve-year-old boy slain in the West Englewood community (see "Reflecting Writing" in chapter 3). I first gave an overview
of our SBM program and then briefly discussed the purpose of the writing activity. Next, each program mentee stepped to the microphone,
stated his name, and read his piece. The members of the audience had
their attention fixed on each young male presenter before them. One
by one, they heard the boys speak of love and loss, of children dying in
city streets, of confusion and rage that violence causes in them, and the
need for social change. After rousing applause, we exited the stage.

At the end of the conference, the boys and I grabbed a bite to eat and
talked about our presentation. They mentioned how fun and exciting it
was to publicly express their writings. They felt that it was important
for people to hear their words because it meant constructing a better

understanding of the lives of young males of color, and I agreed. Despite their impoverished neighborhoods, low academic achievement, and classroom disobedience, these adolescent males were not gun-toting, corner-hustling, loud-talking rebels without a cause. They were human and, in many cases, misunderstood. And it was necessary for people to see and feel their lives, not only as a way of countering skewed images and hyped-up statistics of urban males of color but also to simply understand a representative group of young people.

Another way that I sought to extend student voices beyond the four walls of their school was to arrange a student presentation at a local university. The presentation would be in front of a class of preservice teachers going into public education. On the one hand, I felt that the trip would instill a sense of curiosity and initiative for those boys who were not thinking about higher education. On the other hand, I felt that by hearing students talk about their educative experiences, these particular teachers would be more informed of how to teach and reach students of color.

The boys started off their presentation by reading some of their poetry, personal narratives, and hip hop pieces. Soon after, we briefly went over what our SBM program was and how it functioned as a class in the school environment. We then gave an example of one of our activities. We used an enlarged copy of a newspaper photo that showed the destruction of the New York World Trade Center towers from the September 11, 2001, terrorist attacks. The teachers were asked to write down their thoughts and feelings about the incident. As they wrote, playing in the background were two songs: the first was Sting's "Fragile" and the second was John Lennon's "Imagine." After the second song, we asked the teachers to read their written responses. Some vehemently questioned the terrorist attacks, others wondered about their safety and future, some were driven to tears as they struggled to read.

The final minutes of the presentation were left open for any classroom questions or comments. One teacher asked, "How does a suburban teacher reach students who have grown up in the inner city?" In their responses, the boys generally concluded that teachers, regardless of where they are from, need to try to understand all students and the different issues they face. By doing this first, teachers can teach things that relate to student life. For these boys, teaching is not so much about where the teachers are from or the color of their skin but rather how they reach out to students.

When a voice is heard it can be an empowering experience. An essential part of expressing oneself in a public space is the provision of access. Access not only means entering but also gaining control—control over one's life and the surroundings. The use of public space serves in the betterment of the Self and of others. Having their critical voices heard, in a place where such youth expressions are rarely articulated, provided the boys with a genuine sense of access and influence. Perhaps, from their words, they changed a person's perception of young people from negative to positive. Conceivably, in the face of their own evolving world, the boys themselves were instrumental in their own transformation, adaptation, and renewal.

BRIDGING THE GAP BETWEEN TEACHERS AND STUDENTS

Creating an in-school space to help boys manage their in- and out-of-school lives could be considered pointless if mentors do not engage in helping students relate to their teachers and vice versa. In-school spaces can be quite ineffective if they do not seek to bridge the gap between SBM spaces and classroom life. Thus, mentors must also serve mentees by advocating for them.

Often, there exists a kind of static or disconnect between students and teachers and a struggle for power. In the school setting, mentors can serve as advocates for youth by talking with them individually or in groups about their lives, classroom situations, and feelings toward teachers and administrators. Although there are programs where teachers serve as advocates, students often have classroom issues in which they feel more comfortable talking with an outside party. In this instance, school-based mentors show their support by not only listening to student concerns and discussing ways of dealing with classroom

situations, but also asking students if they need intervention or media-
tion of a conflict between themselves and teachers or administrators.

Another dimension of the "static" that exists between students and
school staff is the lack of understanding that teachers and administrators have of their students. As mentioned in chapter 2, teachers sometimes have dissimilar backgrounds and have no idea or concept of what
their students are going through on a daily basis. The personal barriers
existing between individuals are based on perceived differences either
socially, politically, economically, or culturally. From either perspective, teachers are not in a close enough position with students to recognize and understand student behaviors, concerns, dialect, or interests.
This social distance can negatively affect the ways teachers teach and
students learn and interact.

In this circumstance, school-based mentors also serve as advocates
for students by informing teachers of what they are consciously (or
unconsciously) misreading in student ability, intention, behavior, and
aptitude. SBM programs provide a bridge for those social and cultural
gaps that exist in schools by affording teachers another interpretation
of what they are seeing from their students. Offering teachers a wider
lens to look through allows for greater insight into how to see, hear,
and reach young people. With this added information, a better relationship can develop between the teacher and the student, leading to
improved student attitudes toward school, higher levels of achievement
and self-esteem, and a decline in discipline referrals and removals.

Teachers cannot work in isolation. In trying to reach and relate to as
many aspects of the child as possible, the effort between teachers and
mentors must be a concerted one. On the one hand, teachers need to
be informed as to what their students are experiencing in and outside
of the classroom. Conversely, mentors also need to have a knowledge
base of what educators experience and know about their students.

Some years ago I was mentoring a group of high-school students. In
one of our group sessions, a student was acting out in class by throwing
balls of paper and yelling across the room. A couple of times I asked
the young man to settle down. After my third request, he threw up both

his hands and stormed out of the classroom. Days later, I was informed by his special education teacher that he was dealing with a host of issues: he had come from a family where he was the youngest of ten siblings (three of his older brothers were all incarcerated)—as the baby of the family he was allowed to do whatever he wanted, including running the streets late at night; he was a member of a local gang; he had been arrested numerous times; he was frequently suspended from school; he had recently been labeled with Attention-Deficit Hyperactivity Disorder and was being pulled out of his regular classroom; he had grade point average of 1.0 on a 4.0 scale.

Not having prior knowledge of any of these issues, I only saw his present and outward behavior. Not knowing what he was experiencing and feeling because of his life circumstances, I vocalized my frustration in front of the class, which further evoked his defiance. However, with teacher partnership, I learned more about this young man's personal and academic situation. Days later, when he returned to the SBM program, he and I spoke one-on-one. Our communication was more compassionate and we both came to an agreement regarding the need for respect that we both clearly wanted to have.

Partnerships between teachers and mentors can function to circumvent those classroom crises that occur on a regular basis (e.g., student apathy, low academic achievement, and antisocial behavior). Genuine support, from administrators and teachers, is crucial in order for SBM programs to truly impact student life. These programs hold the potential to bridge the cultural and social gaps that often exist between teachers and students. SBM programs must feel that, in assisting students, their efforts are collaborative in nature and not competitive. Competition between mentors and teachers will only add to the pervasive dysfunction that already exists within American schools. Addressing all the needs and concerns of students requires as many helping hands as possible. In short, mentors and school staff must all be on the same page.

In ending this section, I would be remiss if I did not note that it is hypocritical for schools to acquire the assistance of an SBM program that seeks to empower students if the school's policy and curriculum functions to disempower them. I have worked with young people to assist them in developing ways of understanding the classroom environment and intelligently communicating with teachers for the sake of bettering their learning experience. Yet some teachers can be unwilling to return the same respect that they so often demand from their students. And, in many instances, the supportive advice that other mentors and I have given students, as well as the actions that students have taken based on that advice, subsequently becomes pointless and impotent.

Given that schools are traditionally autocratic in nature and designed to create an abiding citizenry, it is improbable that students will ever become genuinely empowered while they are in them. Nevertheless, until we as a thoughtful society choose to restructure the entire educational system, there must be interventions set in place that help students become critical thinkers and active participants in their own world.

For students, the schooling experience is more than just about what the teacher is teaching. It is also about understanding oneself in relation to the larger world. Thus, mentors, parents, educators, and administrators must work together to encourage the free expression of student ideas and feelings, the fostering of creative activities, the development of analytical thinking, and the enhancing of mental tools used for reasoning. Through our combined efforts we can strengthen our children and help them achieve their fullest potential and life aspirations.

MENTORING STUDENTS OUTSIDE OF SCHOOL

Providing out-of-school forums for young males of color to communicate their lives not only provides them with public access and agency, but it also affords them a chance to develop deeper relationships with mentors. Undoubtedly, young males need other adult figures in their lives to talk to besides a parent or guardian. Parents are often unaware of, or have very little time to notice, the personal issues faced by boys. Without someone to speak to or help guide them, young males of color can lose their way in the uncertainty of daily dilemmas and challenges.

To help support them, mentors can act as surrogate uncles, supplementing the role of parents. From this additional support these boys have a greater chance of staying on the right track and developing and achieving life goals.

For males of color, the importance of having someone to talk to about day-to-day affairs cannot be expressed enough. From my mentoring experiences, conversations with young people are occasionally one way, where I merely function as a soundboard for them to voice their thoughts, problems, and emotions. At other times, they require my feedback. Yet in some cases their problem is urgent and they need immediate advice and viable alternatives to their situation.

An instance of this occurred a few summers ago. One of my mentees (whom I will refer to as Calvin) phoned me in the middle of the night after facing a potentially deadly situation. Moments earlier, he had left a neighborhood party and was making his way home. On his way, Calvin was confronted by a man with a gun. The man told him to walk on the other side of the street. Valuing his life, Calvin complied. When he arrived home, he called me.

In our conversation, Calvin expressed deep and conflicting thoughts over the incident. He questioned his decision to take another way home: "Why couldn't I walk on that side of the street? It's just as much my right as it is anyone else's." "Did I walk away too soon?" "Should I have fought him?" "Am I a coward?" In that late-evening hour, Calvin needed someone to talk to, someone to help him make sense of his distressing situation, someone to aid him in understanding those life circumstances that tug and pull at one's sense of morality.

Youth need someone to take notice of their lives and assist them with problems that they are facing, and a mentor can act in the capacity of a soundboard, a trusted adviser, or both. For me, being there for Calvin and listening to his issues was a mentor's labor of love. Calvin's street-corner incident left him wrestling with ideals of male bravado versus self-preservation. By first receiving a safe moment in which to vent, he was able to release sensitive thoughts and feelings surrounding his experience. Afterward, we were able to discuss, in a logical manner, the options (e.g., physical confrontation or retaliation) as well as the potentially harmful consequences of not walking away. At the end of our talk, I truly believe that Calvin felt much better about his decision and about himself.

This anecdote demonstrates the point that young people should have a wise and objective adult in their lives to listen to them, guide them, counsel them, and provide them with, among other things, emotional and psychological support. Given the mixture of social messages that saturate their lives (vis-à-vis television, magazines, movies, parental/peer influences, school curriculum, etc.), children and adolescents need someone to help them understand these varying perspectives within the delicate framework of their own evolving identities.

When young people are mentored both in and outside of the school environment, they find support in navigating their present world, as well as making the sometimes difficult transition into adulthood. Mentoring relationships based on friendship, trust, and mutual respect place young folks in the favorable position of being able to open up, reveal who they are, and express the kind of person that they wish to be. The freedom to share what they know and to communicate what they feel affords them a social experience that is conducive to healthy human development and overall well-being.

BRIDGING THE GAP BETWEEN SCHOOL AND HOME LIFE: COLLABORATIONS WITH MENTORS, PARENTS, AND COMMUNITIES

Working with mentees outside of school also provides mentors an opportunity to develop meaningful relationships with parents. In my own experiences, I have been invited to family gatherings, where I was treated like a member of the family. By being present in family affairs, I was able to build trusting and dependable relationships with mothers, fathers, grandparents, aunts, and uncles. If there was a personal issue with their child, families knew that they could call me and talk about it. From school issues to teenage rebellion and from neighborhood problems to adolescent aspirations, I was there to assist. Almost certainly, a part of being an effective mentor means having the approval and confidence of the parents.

Supportive relationships between mentors and parents are also fundamental where parents are unsuccessful in communicating their concerns and feelings about their child to teachers. In this instance, school-based mentors have the potential to serve as an added bridge between the home and the school. For example, I was developing a mentoring relationship with a young man who was being expelled from his school due to his constant low grade point average and his accumulated school absences. As a result of the diminished communication between his home and school, I was then asked by the young man's mother to step in and serve as an advocate for her son.

In a meeting with his homeroom teacher and the school's principal, I was able to reveal other dimensions of the young man (e.g., his late-night work hours and his responsibility for taking care of his infant child) that they were not seeing. My role and perspective, as a mentor, helped to shed light on what they construed as the boy's apathy toward schooling. Subsequently, they allowed the young man to stay another semester provided that his grades and attendance would improve. Because of my relationship with this young man and his mother, I was able to mitigate a situation that may have otherwise ended undesirably for both.

Less than amicable relationships between parents and teachers date back to the earliest days of schooling. In some cases, these relationships result in communication gaps between the two parties. Rifts between teachers and parents are due to differences in customs, language, socioeconomic backgrounds, and the intellectual inadequacy that some parents feel when dealing with teachers and the school system. When relationships are antagonistic, sometimes parents will only hear a teacher's poor evaluation of their child's behavior or academic performance. In other cases, parents withdraw altogether from their child's schooling experience. By bringing their own perspective, mentors can communicate another interpretation of the student. This provides both teachers and parents a wider lens to look through when assessing and relating to the student. Partnerships between school representatives and family members can lead to increased social and academic support for males of color.

Tightly linked with school support is the need for strong community relationships and collaborations. This is essential to the success of both school- and community-based mentoring programs. Programs that work in isolation, rather than building partnerships with other community members and youth agencies, limit themselves. In order to understand the various environments and needs of Latino and African American males, mentoring programs need to recognize, and be in touch with, those persons and structures that play a significant role in their lives. For example, what is the student's home life like? Is he experiencing difficulty with a class or teacher? What extracurricular activities is the student involved in? Being familiar with these issues grants greater insight to guiding mentoring programs so that they can appropriately address and help relieve the problems that these young males cope with daily.

Through collaborative community efforts, mentoring males of color can extend beyond single agencies and environments (e.g., school, church, community center) and reach into multiple social spaces where they work, play, and live, thus possibly having a greater positive impact on their lives. SBM programs have the greatest chance of success when they can (1) provide a program where students are connected to program goals, can contribute to the program agenda, and are empowered by the entire experience and (2) partner with schools and families, attending to the interests of students while keeping lines of communication open between teachers and parents.

SBM programs ultimately work best when they are consistent and exist within the contextual framework of the school and/or community. Programs that have a good rapport with teachers and staff often have the upper hand in developing and preventing early school failure as opposed to intervening and correcting the problem after students have already proven academically unsuccessful.

SBM programs also work best when they create and maintain open

lines of communication with and between the student and his other
social worlds. Whether the relationships are created with teachers, parents, other students, siblings, or aunts or uncles, the knowledge and
information that these people possess is invaluable, especially when
communication results in a greater understanding of, and assistance to,
the youth. Furthermore, by enlisting these human community
resources, SBM programs can help build viable social networks that aid
in reducing social fragmentation and the loss of community members.

CLOSING REMARKS

Mentoring is a human practice. It is found within our schools, homes,
communities, and places of business. It is practiced, whether we know
it or not, by teachers, parents, principals, family members, and community workers. As we mentor youth, we find that it is a holistic
endeavor that seeks to know and engage them in and outside of school.
To come to know children and adolescents in these spaces, to observe
how they interact, to understand how they negotiate within these
worlds, and to be there to assist them if wanted, is the practice not only
of mentoring but also of loving and understanding young people. This
is a lesson and a practice that can be carried out by anyone and in any
corner of our society.

Helping males of color vent and deal with their personal problems
is the primary focus of this book. However, as I hope the reader has
determined, all young people need someone who genuinely cares about
them and wants to listen to their issues. Youth need to know that it is
their concerns and their lives that are at the heart of the conversation.
Inasmuch as we, as adults, want to direct young folks with our ideas,
values, and ways of being, all children and adolescents need to sense
that the basis of the discussion is genuine, with concern for them and
their betterment.

Unfortunately, the present atmosphere in our public schools, where
we find a majority of Latino and African American males, encapsulates
students in an air devoid of self-knowledge, self-discovery, creativity,
and care. I believe that within each and every youth lies a seed that

waits to burgeon into a sturdy oak. All youth need is the right set of conditions to flourish, grow, and stand firm.

Historically, the issues and concerns of young males of color have existed on the periphery of curriculum design and implementation, and currently they still reside there. As learning professionals we need to resituate these voices and place them in the center of our curriculum discussions and at the focal point of our policymaking decisions. This group must cease being objectified. They are fully human and mirror what we once were and perhaps what we still are: timid, delicate, unsure, anxious, confused, curious, expressive, passionate, ambitious, and hopeful.

For these reasons and others, males of color deserve our care and support. We cannot proceed on their behalf after they have committed some violent or horrific act for attention, resulting in the loss of innocent lives and the heightening of our existing fears. Without delay, we must aspire to hear and see them more clearly, to know that they are redeemable and hold promise. In light of this, I reiterate a few points that were made in previous sections of *Mentoring Young Men of Color*.

First, if we are working within urban schools or any community where males of color reside, it is vital that we are aware of our perceptions of them. For example, mentors and teachers must avoid popularized and inaccurate representations of males of color that brand them as unintelligent, angry, loud, uncontrollable, dysfunctional, or violent. Such widespread characterizations objectify these students and prevent us from opening up our hearts and minds to them.

Hence, one of the challenges for professionals is to see these students as our own children, to mentor them, teach them, care for them, understand them, and communicate with them as if they were our own flesh and blood. This requires us to move beyond the negative imagery and language that surround the lives of Latino and African American males and not view their individual acts as typical of their ethnicity. Instead, we must recognize that each and every child has a strong desire to be independent, to be successful, to feel loved, to actualize their dreams, to help others, to be free, to have fun, to have a voice and for it be respected, and to be understood not as an inner-city or rural youth, but merely as a *youth*.

Second, in order to authentically connect with young males of color, we must learn to appreciate their individual histories, experiences, and perspectives and recognize these as valid sources of knowledge. As we aspire to build healthy partnerships with these boys it is imperative that we as mentors, teachers, counselors, administrators, parents, and researchers be responsive to the culture, language, and learning styles that they possess. Rejecting or ignoring what they value will only result in silent classrooms and oppressive relationships that foster student disillusion, disengagement, and disidentification from the schooling process as a whole. Alternatively, we must learn to favor their voices as they apprise us of their lived realities and individual differences.

By creating spaces of multiple discourses, we can engage males of color in exploring the mixture of thoughts, identities, and ways of knowing that work together to shape our world. I have found that by using the various mentoring methods discussed in this book, the classroom can be transformed into a liberating, learning environment where participants: (1) openly discuss culturally relevant topics and phenomena that impact their daily lives, (2) reveal and release emotionally sensitive issues that regular school curricula may not address or encourage, (3) reflect and act upon personally conflicting situations and labor together or individually to make positive change as they define it, and (4) feel cared for and cared about as a result of being able to freely express their ideas and feelings. This type of space cultivates authentic dialogue and extends the opportunity for mentors, as well as teachers, to genuinely know and understand students without forcing or artificially obtaining student knowledge and experiences (via surveys, questionnaires, inventories, evaluations).

Finally, I want to underscore the importance of helping males of color develop positive attitudes about themselves. As was discussed in earlier sections of *Mentoring Young Men of Color*, identity development for youth of color is exacerbated when fraught by such issues as "at-risk" labeling, hypermasculinity, racial awareness in a predominantly

White society, negative imagery tied to minority status, and low self-esteem. Understanding that attitude is an aspect of identity, it follows that by building healthy attitudes (e.g., self-worth, competence, and resilience) males of color can achieve a sense of direction and personal coherence needed for successful identity formation. Hence, schools and other social institutions need to structure their programmatic endeavors, policies, and curricula within those public spaces where males of color struggle—the school and the community.

The main approach discussed here is that of school-based mentoring (SBM). Mentoring on school sites gives young males the chance to address their problems in their immediacy. As educators realize, all students bring into schools a host of affective issues that impact their behavior as well as their learning. In classrooms where teachers rarely have sufficient time to engage young people in conversations about their in- and out-of-school lives, mentors can serve as a resource for students who need to express the desires and concerns that go unheard or ignored in the classroom. The interpersonal bonds that define mentor–mentee relationships may well assist in reaching into those emotional spaces that teachers cannot see or often have little time to deal with.

School-based mentoring provides students with a safe place to freely express themselves without fear of judgment or admonishment. These youth-focused environments give rise to the removal of psychological and emotional obstructions, while opening a clear passageway to constructive student behaviors and academic success. Through mentoring we can help to build students' self-esteem, resilience, appreciation of their culture, and critical awareness of their community—all in order to gain a positive outlook on life. School-based mentoring can transform the present atmosphere of schools into a medium where young people can construct productive and promising ways of living and envisioning their world.

Similar to teaching, school-based mentoring provides students with the necessary knowledge to meet their developmental needs. Although young people occasionally seek my advice about their education, I mostly find myself sharing life lessons (and in some cases life-saving lessons) with them—a vital curriculum to be used throughout their journey in this world. As a mentor, I believe that it is my responsibility to embrace and nurture their young lives. I serve to not only better their classroom experiences but also their larger lived experiences, which occur far beyond the bricks and mortar of schools.

5

A REAL History Lesson
Part 1: Origins of an
SBM Program

If you would understand anything, observe its beginning and its development.

—Aristotle

In the next two chapters, I present a brief history of the school-based mentoring program entitled REAL (Respect, Excellence, Attitude, and Leadership). This account is largely autobiographical and co-biographical in nature, relying on my own memory and the recollections of several REAL mentors and mentees. As our shared remembrances of the program could make up an entirely separate book itself, this narrative will focus only on REAL's pilot run and its first year as an SBM program. The names of individuals have been changed in the interest of confidentiality.

How did REAL begin? It all started in my first year of graduate school at the University of Illinois at Chicago. I was studying curriculum design and my emerging research interests focused on socially and culturally relevant curricula for students of color. A professor who knew of my scholarly ideas asked me if I might offer some advice to the faculty of Visions, a fledgling charter school. The school was experiencing behavioral and academic problems with its male student body and needed consultation. Although I had no experience as a professional consultant, I decided that I would speak with the school's directors and offer any support that I could.

Visions Charter School (VCS) was founded in 1996 by Linda Peterson and Doris Hart, two former public school teachers who hold the school's charter. At the time, VCS was one of the city's fifteen charter schools. Charters are public schools but are autonomous in creating their own school code, philosophy, and length of school day and year. They can hire their own teachers and set their own salaries. Although they receive partial funding from the city's board of education, a larger portion of their support comes from public and private donations. Charter schools are not required to use public school textbooks or prescribed curricula. Instead, the board of education allows these schools to design curricula they deem appropriate for their student population.

VCS students matriculate from all areas of the city and are selected through a lottery. Doris and Linda prefer to keep the population small with a familial-type atmosphere. In the 2000–2001 academic year, the student body (grades six through twelve) comprised approximately 150 students. On average, class sizes had a student to teacher ratio of 20:1. VCS students are mainly from low to middle socioeconomic status, while teachers are from middle to upper-middle. As with many public and charter schools, VCS students are required to wear uniforms. The attire consists of black slacks, black shoes, and a light blue, long-sleeve dress shirt with the VCS logo stitched in the upper right-hand corner. Students are also allowed to wear VCS's honor roll T-shirts, which bear the names of those students who academically excelled in one particular semester.

Expectations for students are grounded in what the school calls "Positive Living"—a set of twenty-one principles that form the foundation of the school's philosophy. Each grade spends one hour a week engaged in activities that revolve around these tenets. They are: love yourself; recognize only quality work from yourself; be accountable for your actions; search for wisdom; be flexible in your thinking; think decisively; be giving; demonstrate honor and integrity; communicate well; test each other intellectually; have a kind word for others; be sociable; resolve conflicts peacefully; respect differences; support a classmate; use your time sensibly; listen earnestly; be prompt; be prepared; be insightful; be dependable.

The founders of VCS contend that Positive Living holds both students and teachers accountable for their actions. For example, according to the school's 1998–1999 annual report, such tenets as "demonstrate honor and integrity" are used to help students understand the personal deficit they create when they are not completely forthright with themselves, and "communicate well" seeks to encourage articulation and mature two-way conversations between staff members, teachers and students, students and their peers, and parents and teachers.

Outside of their Positive Living philosophy, VCS also promotes the following: VCS offers students mentoring opportunities and internships with city employers from local food companies, hotels, and universities; students are involved with activities that expose them to the community such as field studies, guest speakers, community services, and college tours; VCS has mandatory parent–teacher–student conferences three times annually; and graduating seniors do not receive a diploma unless they are accepted, with funding, to a university or college, enrolled in a trade school, have joined the military, or have acquired a job that is self-supportive.

Before calling Linda, I waited a few days, trying to figure out exactly what to say and what I was actually doing. I had only taught for five years in Chicago's public school system and with that came some reasonable understanding of educational practices, but who was I to offer viable solutions to veteran teachers and administrators? Despite my feelings of inadequacy, I picked up the phone to call her. In our talk, Linda briefly discussed her school's history and the issues that her staff faced. I offered a few ideas that I had read about on culturally relevant curricula, hoping this would satisfy her, but it was not enough. She wanted me to address her staff at an in-service meeting offering practical strategies. As she sounded a bit at the end of her rope, I found it difficult to say no and agreed to go in.

Because I was not entirely confident speaking in front of a group of teachers and suggesting solutions to their problems, I invited three fellow graduate students who had more teaching and consulting experience than I did. One was an assistant principal at a Chicago public school, another was a student of social work and a curriculum consultant, and the other was a published author on schooling and a teacher for several years. After informing each of them of the circumstances surrounding Visions, they kindly agreed to assist me. Our basic plan of action was to first listen and gather teacher concerns. Then, after the in-service, we would evaluate the staff's issues and develop individual responses. I would later report back our entire assessment to Doris and Linda.

On the outside, VCS was a modestly small, two-story, red brick building located only a few miles from Chicago's downtown. Neighboring structures were mostly old warehouses and lofts that were being renovated into high-rise condominiums. In fact, the building housing VCS was formerly a piano warehouse. Behind the school was a desolate lot that was littered with trash and rubble, and a railway bridge, where trains rumbled by daily. The cold, wintry air of January only accentuated the lot's barrenness.

Despite the school's dreary industrial surroundings, VCS was bright on the inside. Large windows in the classrooms and main office brought in huge amounts of sunlight. White lockers lined the first floor hallway. Hanging from the walls were several framed photographs that captured the smiles of students and teachers. As opposed to other high schools, I saw no security guards or metal detectors. I heard no bells or buzzers. The school had none of the above.

The in-service was held on the first floor in the staff lounge. All of the teachers from the middle and high school were present. Being that it was a small school, there were a total of about ten teachers on staff. Eight of them were White and only two were African American. Their ages ranged from early thirties to late forties. Doris and Linda were both White and in their mid-thirties.

My colleagues and I commenced the meeting by introducing ourselves. The staff then went around the table, stating their names and the courses that they taught. Next, we opened up the floor to their issues. What initially started out as a subdued roundtable of teachers soon became an energized forum of voices. Tidal waves of questions rushed toward me and my colleagues. The main issues that swept the room related to student behavior and academic achievement. We were told that an overwhelming number of Visions' high-school boys were making failing to low passing grades. Girls comprised the majority of students on the honor rolls in previous semesters. Moreover, numerous boys were incurring heavy infractions leading to in and out of school suspensions.

Linda added that Visions was nearly 80 percent African American, less than 20 percent Latino, and approximately 5 percent White. With respect to the racial disparity between students and staff, some teachers believed that their gender and ethnicity played a role in the classroom relationships that they had with many of their male students. One of the primary concerns that these teachers expressed was their need to have a more diversified staff for their young men to identify with.

After more than an hour of discussion, the in-service came to a close. Although I sensed that the staff expected quick and easy answers to come out of that meeting, I told them that my colleagues and I would discuss what was said and work to develop strategies to assist them. About a week passed before I phoned Linda. I informed her that my group came to the general conclusion that, among other things, the boys would likely benefit from an in-school mentoring program. Linda expressed her appreciation for our visit and told me that she would go over our recommendation with the staff. I thanked her for having us and we said our good-byes. It was no less than two months later before Linda called me back. Before I could get the word "hello" out of my mouth, she pointedly asked, "So when are you coming in to start this mentoring program?"

THE PILOT RUN

In late February I returned to Visions. Linda had successfully convinced me to extend my support by helping them create an in-school program for the high-school boys. Upon arriving for an after-school meeting, I discovered that Linda had acquired the assistance of two other volunteers. One was Luis Jimenez, a twenty-six-year-old father of two students attending the school. He was about 6′3″ and built like a football player. The other was Mel Jackson, a business entrepreneur in his mid-thirties, who was also active in the surrounding community. Mel was heavyset, about six feet tall, and dark brown in complexion. We were told that Alfred Simmons, the only male African American teacher at VCS, would later join us in this venture. Linda felt that Alfred was a good candidate as a mentor, being that the students related to him. She then handed us a three-page document developed by her and her staff that summarized their suggestions regarding the mentoring program. She went through the mission statement with us briefly:

Brotherhood Organization for Support and Success (BOSS)

Mission Statement: This team of male students will come together to build strong community and discuss a range of male issues. The team will meet to build personal esteem and instill characteristics of leadership.

At Visions we recognize the problem and are committed to turning this cycle around. BOSS aims to create men who contribute to a better community, communicate their ideas intelligently and learn to love who they are. We need to get our young men to see themselves in positions of power.

VCS intends to help make this happen within our young men through the following strategies:

- BOSS will provide open enrollment for boys grades 9–12
- Monday sessions 2x per month 3:45–5:30?
- Students participate in Team Building Retreat / trust building
- Students exposed to guest speakers
- Students attend rich cultural or "just for fun" field studies . . . movies, ball games, symphony, jazz concert

- Students engaged in role play and small / large group discussions regarding various issues effecting them

After Linda left the room, Mel, Luis, and I talked. We mulled over the program's purpose, infusing our own ideas into BOSS's objective and mission statement. Mel, from an entrepreneurial perspective, felt that we could build a business to umbrella the staff's strategies. He mentioned selling a product called "Tea of the Earth," along with organic fruits and vegetables. We then discussed an orientation date for the students, some survey questions to ask them, and an agenda for the program among other things. Ideas for the program's agenda included issues that we felt boys needed to talk about: the importance of education, the value of a dollar, peer pressure, business entrepreneurship, teen sex and pregnancy, how to treat a woman, alcohol and drug abuse, and the meaning of friendship.

We were also not entirely fond of Linda's initial name for the program, BOSS, so we came up with several alternatives: Brotherhood Forum, ROYAL (Respecting Our Young African Americans and Latinos), REALM (Reclaiming and Educating African American and Latino Males), and REALITY (Respecting and Educating African Americans and Latinos in Their Youth). The three of us agreed that the name of the program had to be something catchy and current, therefore we tentatively called it REAL (Respecting and Educating African Americans and Latinos).

Being that REAL was to be held every other week for an hour after school, we thought of some persuasive ways for getting the boys involved. Mel figured that making money could be a main attraction. Hence, we made one aspect of the program business finance and management. Students would take on the roles of workers, executive officers, and directors. They would select products to be sold and services to be rendered. However, in keeping aligned with the staff's ideas, we made the other part of the program a focus on student-affective issues. REAL in this regard would serve as a roundtable where students and mentors could interact and discuss important life issues.

Over the course of about two weeks, Mel and I passed out flyers to the high-school boys, notifying them of the program and its start date. Additionally, Doris and Linda arranged for the boys and girls to be split up, during their Positive Living time, so that Mel and I could do informal presentations with the boys. In our talks with students, we informed them that REAL would be an all-male program, and it was going to focus on entrepreneurship and building brotherhood in the school. We told them that if they had any ideas on how to make money, they should bring them to the first session.

REAL held its first meeting on April 10 at 3:45. Out of a possible sixty male high-school students, only three showed up. They were juniors. In addition to them, there was me, Mel, and Alfred. Our fourth mentor, Luis, was a no-show. Apparently, a week before REAL's first meeting, he had taken his children out of VCS. At the time, my inquiries into his leaving went unanswered. This first meeting lasted only twenty minutes and involved everyone introducing themselves and stating why they were there. All of the boys stated that they were interested in starting a business and wanted to know where to begin. Mel assured them that they would learn some business techniques while in the program. At the end of the session, he asked the boys to bring some of their friends to the next scheduled meeting.

April 24 marked our second session. Before the meeting began, Doris had ushered in seven freshmen who had been involved in discipline problems earlier that day. I thought to myself what a huge mistake that was. Now these students were going to see the program as a kind of punishment rather than an opportunity or reward. Despite the implications of Doris's action, the company of these boys was welcomed. Strolling in behind them were a few other students. Alfred was absent. Our attendance reached twelve that day.

At the outset of the meeting, the boys clowned around and made jokes about each other, taking very little notice of me or Mel. One kid, Jay Guevara, decided to draw graffiti art on pieces of notebook paper. His small, round glasses and tidy appearance gave off a scholarly impression. On the other side of the room was Lee Camacho entertaining his peers by vocalizing hip hop lyrics, while his sidekick, Calvin Johnson, banged beats on a desk for him to rap over. Lee's long, uncombed Afro, rumpled school uniform, and multiple silver neck chains definitely gave him a rough edge. Calvin looked more like Lee's opposite, with his neatly cropped haircut and smoothly pressed shirt and pants. Mel and I asked them and the rest of the class to settle down. After a few a minutes, we finally got their attention.

We first had the boys go around the room, introduce themselves, and state why they were in attendance. Most of them openly admitted that they were there because of their disciplinary infraction. Afterward, Mel began his discussion on products and services. He tried to get the boys to brainstorm products to sell and ways of providing a service to the local community. Lee was the first to speak. He asked if REAL was going to be a hip hop club. The class responded with laughter. Mel good-humoredly replied no and then returned the subject back to products and services.

One student proposed that we sell audio CDs around the city. Others joined in and offered ideas such as selling mix tapes, cellular phones, candy, or laundry detergent, and designing T-shirts, jackets, and socks. Expressing that these things were beyond the program's reach, Mel pushed for something more feasible like his inside connection to the "Tea of the Earth" product. The boys voted against it. The same student who mentioned selling CDs put forth the idea of having a car wash. Some of the boys grunted when they heard the idea, so we took a vote. A slim majority of hands wanted to do the car wash. And with that as our elected student project, the meeting adjourned.

As for the seven boys receiving disciplinary punishment by attending REAL, in our next Monday meeting, none of them returned. From my attendance sheets dated throughout the pilot program, none of them ever came back. In an interview, I asked Lee and Jay their thoughts about that session.

Lee: When I was first introduced to REAL, I didn't find it interesting because I didn't know that much about it. I thought it was a boys club—

guys go hang out and talk about various things. The first time I was in REAL, we were talking about having a car wash. I wasn't cool with doing a car wash, and I felt like I was being told to do it and not asked. I think the views in REAL were different then. I think Mr. Jackson had more of a parental type view.

Jay: It kind of caught my attention because we were talking about the business aspect of making money. The thought of me becoming an entrepreneur was pretty interesting—the things that one can do, creativity, and building some type of success off of that. That kind of drew me into it. At first, I thought that this could be good for me, that it could take me somewhere. But as time went on, I kind of went with the crowd. They weren't feeling it; they didn't want to wash cars, and I wanted to talk about things deeper than money. So, I ended up ditching the program.

With the month of May approaching, and attendance being as modest as it was, Mel, Alfred, and I decided to open up the program to the middle-school boys. Within grades six through eight, there were about thirty males. We believed that we could possibly pull a third of them in. By including the younger guys, it would be a way to not only boost our attendance but also draw greater attention to the program. We informed Doris, Linda, and the middle-school teachers of our plan. They all thought it was a good idea. We asked the teachers to inform the lower-grade boys as to when and where REAL would meet. In our third session, only one middle-school student showed up—a sixth grader. Also there were the three regularly attending juniors.

In the meeting Mel went over what he called "business protocol and standards." It mainly dealt with the rules and responsibilities of workers in the car wash. He also went over the concepts of manpower and production. Later, he asked our small group of attendees to come up with items needed for the car wash. We listed sponges, rags, towels, air fresheners, tire cleaner fluid, wax, buckets, and car soap.

Afterward, Mel asked the four boys to select "job titles" from a prepared list. Being offered were the positions of president of REAL, vice president, vice president of marketing, and director of human resources. Paris Brandy, a junior, volunteered to take the position of REAL's president. In doing so, his first order of business was asking members to help him develop a few principles that would help guide the program. Paris presented the argument that if REAL was partly about creating young leaders for the business world, then it needed words that did not solely focus on Latino and African American tenets. Agreeing with his statement, we used our remaining time to come up with the following four principles to direct program goals: respect, excellence, attitude, and leadership. The meanings of these words, as they would relate to the program, were later expanded on in our first program pamphlet:

> *Respect*—for my parents, teachers, business associates, fellow students, and myself
>
> *Excellence*—to work harder on academics and strive to be a better student by example
>
> *Attitude*—improve myself and work on anger, maturity, responsibility, and commitment by staying positive
>
> *Leadership*—I will conduct myself as a leader and I will be a team player. I am practicing for success

Included in the pamphlet was the program's mission statement:

> REAL (Respect, Excellence, Attitude, and Leadership) is a supplementary education and mentoring program designed to help provide male students from ages 11–18 with life skills that are considered necessary for success both in and out of school. The mission of the program is two-fold: (1) to develop positive academic, emotional, and intellectual growth through problem solving activities and classroom discussions, and (2) to expose youth to practical real life business skills through a process of researching, creating, and organizing an actual business. Using a teamwork approach, students plan and execute, with the assistance of adult facilitators, various marketing productions.

Although the program relatively engaged the small group of boys that we had, I felt that it was leaning more toward the business side of the curriculum. In my thinking, there was nothing wrong with having a few sessions on marketing strategies but with a balance and an inclination toward other topics that students wanted to talk about.

As mentors, we were not calling enough attention to student affective issues. I partly blame myself for this because, at that time, I wasn't completely sure what REAL should have been about. I didn't know exactly how to teach or reach these young men as a mentor. In the absence of my own confidence and clarity, I sat back while Mel took on a determined leadership role. Where REAL was supposed to be a combination of business and emotional growth, it became what Linda later called "Business 101." Our meetings continually stressed the business venture of the car wash—something our small group later dubbed "The REAL Deal Car Wash."

By early May, REAL attendance still showed no signs of increasing. As a way to bring more students into the program, Mel decided to partner with a Parma Elementary School, located only a few blocks north of VCS. The school's principal relished the idea of the REAL Program. At our May 15 meeting, she allowed her middle-school boys, with permission from their parents, to come up to Visions after school and participate in REAL. At that meeting, we had fifteen boys in attendance; twelve were from Parma. In later sessions, a bulk of our attendance was made up of the Parma boys. Linda and Doris were not totally opposed to this but wondered why their students were not in the majority. In spite of this initial thrust of Parma students, our overall attendance continued to wane. By mid-June, program membership consisted of seven students; only two were from Visions.

By the close of the school year and well into the summer, "The REAL Deal Car Wash" had started to take shape. We were hosting three car washes that would operate on Saturdays throughout the month of July. Mel prepared a flyer and distributed it to school staff, students, parents, and members of the surrounding community.

This weekend please come out and support REAL's 1st production
JULY 8th 11:00 a.m. to 3:00 p.m.
THE 1st REAL Deal Car Wash – A "SPONGE-CLEAN ONLY"
HAND CAR WASH & Special Services
$5 for outside/$7 for in and outside jobs
Other Special Services Include
*Armor-All Clean Tires and Dashboards!
White Wall Tires and Rims!
Spot-Clean Rug Shampoo-while u wait!
*Windex Clean All Windows
Ice Cold *Caffeine Free, Herbal TEA OF THE EARTH!
Ice Cold Lemonade from H&S Purified Water . . . from scratch!
. . . Popcorn, Chips, *Portman Cookies and more! GET IN HERE!!!!

All three car washes took place in VCS's parking lot. We ran a hose from the school's kitchen and out of a ground-floor window. Cars entered and exited the parking lot in a circular route. Mel and I donated all of the supplies and snacks. Between eight and ten of the Parma students showed up for all three events. Invariably, there were two to three VCS boys participating. Our grand total from all three car washes amounted to $615.00, including customer donations. Mel deposited the earnings into a "community organization" account. The money was to be used for future student outings and projects.

At the first car wash I was introduced to Larry Skylar, a friend of Mel's and a resident of the area. At the time, Larry—African American and in his early forties—was the lead fitness reporter for a local news station. He commented that he liked how we were working with the young men and wanted to be a part of the program. Needing his assistance, Mel, Alfred, and I agreed to bring him on board. I asked Larry to recall his thoughts on REAL's pilot run.

Originally it was Mel Jackson who I had gotten some emails from about starting off this car wash thing and he asked me to be a part of that. During those car washes, I met Horace and Alfred, and it evolved from there. It was definitely a positive thing which made me want to be a part of it. I thought that working with REAL would help me understand the world in which my own kids were growing up in.

In the car washes, I could see the kids reacting to a situation where they had responsibilities and had to work together as a team. That team work was kind of hard sometimes because it was almost like they wanted to outshine each other, which is a good thing when you can manage it. I could also see some of those kids taking so much pride in the work that they were doing and taking pride from our response of giving them a pat on the back. It's so important to get positive reinforcement from role models. The kids definitely reacted to us in a positive way.

Late July marked the last scheduled car wash, and perhaps not a moment too soon. Apparently, one of the Parma students used a steel wool pad to scrub one of the cars. Mel decided to pay for the car's repainting out of his pocket to avoid depleting program funds. To make matters worse, the program was being accused of using children to make money for the mentors. The allegation came from an irate parent who decided to attend the REAL meeting that followed the last car wash.

Firmly holding her son's arm, the parent marched in and planted herself at the opposite end of the table from Mel. Mel started the meeting by stating the total amount of money accrued from all three car washes. Before he was able to say much more than that, the woman cut him off and adamantly demanded that her son be paid for his work. Mel calmly explained to her that the money was put into a collective account for student trips and activities. Not wanting to hear any excuses, she threatened to inform the police and other parents. She then grabbed her son and one of his friends and stormed out of the room. I thought to myself, "Wow. This is all over before it even had a chance to begin."

In early August, the woman's dreadful warning was realized. Although she did not pursue the threat of going to the police, a majority of the Parma Elementary students were absent in our final two summer sessions. REAL's pilot program ended with just four boys left. Three were from Parma and one was from VCS.

Later that summer, I asked several VCS boys about the car wash project. According to them, it was not the best strategy for drawing students into the program. They gave three key reasons. (1) It turned out that car wash idea had been done repeatedly by VCS in past school fundraisers. Students knew that the amount of money earned was going to be minimal and thus not worth their time and effort. In short, they did not see the car wash as a means for putting "real" money into their pockets. (2) Some of the older boys already had jobs, so there was nothing much financially that a car wash could offer them. (3) The car washes were held at the school, on Saturdays, during summer break—a place and a time when working outside in almost triple-digit heat was far less appealing than hanging out with friends by the lakefront.

As for our low attendance, these boys stated that REAL was "inconveniently" scheduled after school—a time when they were rushing out of school doors to find much-needed freedom. Moreover, REAL was scheduled every other Monday. That length of time between sessions was not consistent enough, particularly in the life of busy teenagers. I would see many of the boys leaving VCS after school. When I asked them if they were coming to the meeting, they would proffer excuses like, "I forgot there was a meeting," "Sorry, I've got a lot of homework to do," "I have to baby-sit," or "I'm on my way to work." With respect to their various reasons, REAL needed to be scheduled at a time that would not conflict with students' after-school activities.

All in all, REAL's pilot run was a learning experience that progressively gave me a sense of clarity and confidence. Even though Mel pushed the boys to talk about their ideas, it was mostly for the sake of starting a business. We rarely helped them navigate stressful or potentially violent situations in their classrooms or neighborhoods. We hardly, if ever, invited them to talk about their teachers, their school, their home life, their communities, or their friends. Ultimately, if not unfortunately, the entrepreneur side of the program took precedence—a facet that obviously had very little appeal to these students.

6

A REAL History Lesson Part 2: A Quest for Realness

REAL is a medium of expression for the previously unexpressed.
                              —Paris Brandy (REAL member)

As I sat in REAL during the months of its pilot run, I took copious notes on what students said and did, paying close attention to their interests, perspectives, and expectations. The more familiar I became with the boys, during this time, the easier it was for me to understand why REAL did not attract them the way that I and others expected it to. Likewise, I became more conscious of how the school's organization (e.g., scheduling of classes, disciplinary codes, the school's staff) framed the school's culture. With this understanding, it became easier for me to see how the program might work if it was made over and reintroduced.

During the last two weeks of August I sat down and thought about different ways of revamping the program. Personally, it was not enough for me to end this experience with memories of bored students sitting in meetings, an outraged parent, and a car scrubbed with a scouring pad. Given these lackluster episodes, I didn't want myself or the other mentors to give up on the program. I genuinely believed that, if given a second chance, REAL could properly assist the young men at Visions. We had to thrust it into the new school year being more captivating and student-centered.

Before going back to the drawing board, my first thought was to simply ask the boys what they wanted to do and then develop a curriculum around their responses. However, I knew that the VCS's directors would never go for that. Doris once told me that sometimes students need to be led to water in order for them to drink it. I knew that if REAL was going to be instituted inside Visions, it had to have a formal curriculum that was going to be both agreeable and practical to school staff. It also had to stimulate their male students. It needed to be, as Linda put it, something to "change male student apathy toward schooling." What is more, the other adult facilitators had to find it appealing and worth their time.

Initially, I reflected on REAL's pilot run—more specifically, the day Doris brought in the seven boys into our classroom. Why so many discipline infractions in one day at such a small school? What caused it? Was it the boys? Was it the teachers? Was it the school? If the staff wanted their "young men to see themselves in positions of power" (see BOSS mission statement), then why force them into a REAL meeting as a form of disciplinary action? What was "power" to these teachers, and did their boys share the same outlook? I was pretty sure that they did not.

To further an understanding of all this, I turned to books and educational research journals that examined the socioeconomic plight of males of color, as well as notions of racism, gender, and identity formation in the school setting. In addition to these readings I reflected on my own adolescent years in high school. Perhaps my juvenile experiences mirrored in part what the boys at VCS were going through. Maybe they were experiencing, to some degree, the angst I went through as a high-school student. If so, then the "new REAL model" had to work as an agent against student boredom, frustration, resistance, alienation, aggression, and silencing. Reflecting on my past experiences and looking over my notes from the pilot run, I thought about reinventing the program in two fundamental ways: (1) creating a safe space where male students could express their issues and concerns, and

(2) using arts-based curriculum as a way of encouraging that expression.

Despite the intimacy that their small school promoted, I still believed that the young men of VCS, at some point during their school day, needed to have a moment to exhale away from the often suffocating four walls of the classroom (i.e., no teachers, no female counterparts, no rigid instruction). VCS had a closed campus policy (as do many other charter and public schools), and students did not have the option of leaving school grounds for their lunch break, which was scheduled for only twenty minutes. Also, because of VCS's relatively small class sizes, students would be noticeably missed if they decided to run the risk of cutting class. Thus, REAL would serve as a place for boys to be outside of the classroom but still inside of the school. Preferably, meetings would be held during their school day at a regularly scheduled time.

Yet, as more than a meeting place, REAL would also serve as a space where the young men of Visions could gather, be themselves, and talk about themselves, something lacking in the pilot run. Though students were engaged, and some possibly empowered, by the car wash event, I did not feel that they were renewed by the experience or able to freely express their everyday thoughts and emotions. Thus, for the new school year, REAL would function as a constructive means for relieving anxiety by allowing boys to not only speak about themselves but also to write or dramatize their emotions. If VCS boys were experiencing the same everyday pressures that I underwent as an adolescent, then REAL had to be a place to positively vent their fears and concerns.

After establishing the importance and need for an open and safe environment, I then contemplated the use of an arts-based curriculum. I searched my notes from the pilot program for clues to guide me. Amid the flyers, pamphlets, attendance sheets, and copies of emails, there was a sheet of paper with notes on it dated April 24. This was the session where the seven boys were brought in as a punitive measure. In addition to their comments on sketch artistry, freestyle rhymes, and

REAL as a hip hop club, a student also mentioned selling audio compact discs. What he actually meant was bootlegging music CDs. Even though his idea was never fully addressed at the meeting, it made me think: What if the boys created their own unique journal of writings, with maybe some student drawings inside of it, and then transformed it into an audio CD? Their interest in the arts was obvious. They only needed a vehicle to carry it.

By using the journal and CD concept, the boys of VCS could express their thoughts and emotions through drawing, poetry, and, of course, hip hop. Mel could even help them market it—a combination of the arts and industry. Like the REAL forum itself, the activity had the potential for providing students a conduit to channel and disclose their personal problems and concerns. By supplying them with this artistic medium, the boys of VCS could freely articulate their issues, name their social anxieties, and shape their experiences. The project also had the possibility of altering student apathy toward school. Even though I wanted the boys to come up with their own ideas, this was something that I could present to Mel and Larry, as well as to VCS staff. Once we got the go-ahead from them, we could then ask the boys their thoughts and interests about the project.

VCS IN-SERVICE: TAKE TWO

On a hot and humid August afternoon, I met with Larry and Mel in a coffee shop, a few blocks away from VCS. As the meeting place was central to where they both lived, it also provided a cool shelter from the sweltering outside air. I reminded Mel of the April 24 meeting and how some of the students expressed an interest in the arts. I then ran down the "new" REAL in detail, explaining the objectives behind it. Mel and Larry both agreed that it was a fine idea. Mel affirmed that funds in the REAL account could help finance the project. Even so, we still needed the financial and moral support from VCS. We were all aware of the difficulty in attracting and keeping students after school. So, we agreed that the program had to have at least one hour of in-school time if it was going to be successful.

By mid-September, Visions had already started its fall semester. Doris and I had set up an in-service to go over some ideas surrounding the return of REAL. She was enthusiastic about bringing us back and scheduled us in for a conference later that week. The in-service was held in one of the smaller middle-school classrooms on the first floor. Mel and I showed up promptly at 3:45. Larry could not attend because of a previous engagement.

After going around the table with personal introductions, Mel and I started the meeting off with our evaluation of the pilot run. In combination with the newness of the program and the boys' unfamiliarity with it, we admitted to not having a diversity of activities that more students would be attracted to. I then submitted to everyone a four-page handout of the booklet/CD project. It explained the program's mission and its agenda for the new school year:

> For the 2000–01 academic year, the REAL Youth Program will launch a student generated project entitled, "REAL Voices." This endeavor will serve as an exhibition of creative expressions from the REAL youth as they reflect on the day-to-day high and lows of school and home life. The motivating factors behind this project are three-fold: (1) to actively engage students in cooperative initiatives and exploration, (2) to advance student creativity, individuality, and expression, through the arts and critical education, and (3) to expose teachers, parents, school administrators, and the community at large to the unseen and unheard identities of a representative segment of society's young males of color.

After finishing my overview, I opened up the floor to any feedback. Doris was the first to comment. She stated that the idea was good and that it might get the boys more involved with school. She went on to add that if students were going to do projects other than the booklet/CD, then those activities would need an objective. The other teachers agreed with her. I responded by assuring them that we would create objectives for any independent pursuits. One teacher chimed in and gave me the names of several boys whom he felt had an affinity for rapping and drawing graffiti art. Three of the boys that he mentioned

were Lee, Calvin, and Jay, who I had remembered from the April 24
meeting. According to other teachers, these boys were highly interested
in drawing and rapping and could also influence other students to get
involved with the program.

Next, Mel and I brought up the problems associated with being
scheduled after school. We proposed that REAL might be more effective if we met with students during their school day. A sudden lull filled
the room. I thought this implied the impossibility of our proposition.
Then Doris broke the silence by suggesting that teachers could share
their Positive Living time slot with the program. While some teachers
expressed the need to spend every minute of the day working with their
students, they also felt that an in-school mentoring program could
truly help their boys. At that time, they went over the Positive Living
schedule with us.

Mondays from 10:45–11:45—juniors and seniors; Tuesdays from
12:45–1:30—middle-school grades (six through eight); Wednes-
days—no Positive Living; Thursdays from 10:45–11:45—freshman and
sophomores; Fridays—no Positive Living

According to the schedule, REAL could easily fit into the Tuesday
middle-school slot for one session. Yet, the issue that the staff struggled
with was which day and times all high-school grades could attend, that
is, if the program was given one school day. Having each high-school
grade in one session proved to be an improbable outcome given the
already established class schedules and the school's limited space. Doris
then asked if the program could work with their boys in the morning
and afternoon hours. We told her that it was doable.

It was then finally decided that REAL would meet on the days and
times of Positive Living. For the high-school boys, their participation
would be voluntary. Some of the teachers asserted that the boys should
have a choice between staying in their Positive Living class and going
to REAL meetings. However, the teachers also made the point that the
boys would not be allowed to jump back and forth between the two

classes as it would be disrupting. They maintained that unless they kept a student for Positive Living, they should otherwise be in REAL sessions. As for the middle-school boys, Doris declared that their attendance should be mandatory. She believed that they needed to have mentoring on a regular basis.

Subsequently, I asked Doris and the teachers if they would be further willing to give boys extra credit for attending REAL meetings. I emphasized that the idea might draw in more boys to the program. Another lull pervaded the room. Doris turned to her teachers and asked what they thought. While some were initially hesitant, they agreed that it was good idea as long as the work in REAL related to their respective course subject matter. I thought to myself, "Now, we're rolling."

Before closing the in-service, the staff brainstormed different dates for when REAL could return and present the various projects, as well as a start-up date, to students. We all agreed that the best time to promote the program would be in the second week of October. In that week, teachers would allow us to speak with individual classes during their Positive Living time. Our actual start-up date for program meetings would be the last week of October. There was no mention of financial support from the school. I assumed that REAL would use its internal funds.

BRINGING IT REAL

Throughout the week of October 9, Larry and I met with VCS boys from every grade. Due to unknown circumstances, Mel had to go out of town and was unable to attend any of the promotional sessions. Before each meeting, the girls were taken out of the classroom and situated in either the library or the computer lab. Larry and I introduced ourselves at the beginning of each session, telling the young men a bit about our backgrounds. Many of them remembered me from the previous school year, calling me "the REAL guy." I told them that the program was the same this year but different in some ways. This time we would meet during school hours, we would focus on what they wanted to do, and, if they desired, they could show off their talents and creativity to others.

To give them an idea of the possibilities, I brought in examples of various works that were done by young folks just like them. One artifact was a journal, created by high schoolers. It exhibited their artwork and creative writing. The second artifact was an audio tape recording of a spoken word performance by an unknown poet. The boys were given a transcription of the recording to help them follow along. The poet's pulsating, bass voice held the students captured as he articulated his life growing up on the hard streets of the Bronx in New York City.

After the tape ended, students were given a handout that listed the various projects that REAL was offering. One page showed an illustration of a T-shirt with the title of the program written across it. The second discussed the booklet/CD illustration. The third and final page was left blank and asked the students to provide other ideas that they wanted to explore. At the very bottom of this last sheet, highlighted with an orange marker, were the words "extra credit!!" I informed students that their program projects could serve as extra credit in classes that they were not doing so well in. Students invariably became excited when they saw this option before them. Many of them talked about the classes that they needed extra credit in. Other boys walked around the room and conversed with classmates about their project ideas.

During the final minutes of each session, students jotted down their proposed ideas for program projects or selected one or two of my suggestions. Many of the boys, both in middle and high school, were enthusiastic about pursuing the projects of drawing illustrations for T-shirts and making the booklet/CD. Others proposed producing and selling a REAL newspaper, creating a REAL website, having a football team, and making a video about the program. Larry and I asked the boys to write down the way in which they planned to make their project a reality. An overwhelming majority wrote that in order for these projects to happen, they needed to attend REAL meetings. As students turned in their responses, Larry and I informed them that the program was officially starting next week and if they wanted to accomplish all their ideas, then they had to attend the meetings. From their enthusiasm, especially from the middle-school boys, they were geared to go.

Days before our official start-up I e-mailed Mel to verify once more his schedule in the coming weeks. I already knew that Larry would be able to help out with the middle-school boys in the afternoon. However, Mel's unexpected trip out of town made me slightly question his availability. Now that we had an in-school schedule, and a greater part of the high-school boys were positively responding to the program projects, we all had to be consistent. In his e-mail response, Mel stated, "I am committed and you can count on me except when I have to go out of town (I am out of town again from Wed. afternoon 10/25–10/28)."

In another e-mail correspondence, I sent Mel and Larry an overview of what I thought the first week could look like. As in the previous week of promotions, we would present each grade with the same format. We would go over the significance of the words within the program's acronym and ask students to relate these words to their own lives. I also expressed the importance of building a respectful and safe classroom environment for the sake of getting students to open themselves up to us. A part of this was letting students know that REAL was independent of the school staff. Whatever they were to say and do, within reason and without harm to others, would be between them and us. With any substantial time remaining, we would break students into groups based on their project interests. From their response sheets, a majority of the middle- and high-school boys wanted to pursue the booklet/CD, design T-shirts, and shoot videos. Receiving no objections from either Mel or Larry, I took this as the go-ahead plan.

In the Monday and Thursday meetings with the high school, the boys and I met on the second floor in VCS's library. Being that all classrooms were in use at this time (and VCS has no gym or auditorium), REAL high school meetings were to be held there for the duration of the school year. The library was relatively small, only accommodating an estimated twelve to fifteen students. Despite its size, shelves were lined with a plethora of books, magazines, and a couple of volumes of encyclopedias. Before each session, I took the liberty of spreading out the chairs and tables just in case there was a high student turnout.

At 10:45, second period ended. Filling the hallways was the usual frivolity that comes when students are let out of class. They were given about five minutes to go to their locker or to the bathroom and make it promptly to their next class. On each day, I was eager to see how many boys would make their way to the library. In the Monday session with the juniors and seniors, twelve students showed up. There were only three seniors present—these were the juniors from last year who participated in REAL's pilot run. On Thursday, there were ten freshmen and eight sophomores. Three of the sophomores were the infamous Jay, Calvin, and Lee.

For the first half of each session, I asked students to go around the room, introduce themselves, and state why they were there. Some responded that they were there to initiate their projects. Some admitted that they wanted the offered extra credit. A few others, who were not at the promotional meetings, said that they were there to discover what REAL was actually about.

I started off by informing the boys that REAL was a time and a place for them to come and hang out. If they were tired of being in the classroom, then they could come to REAL and talk about whatever they wanted to. The program was not there for teachers. REAL was their time and their space—it belonged to them. I went on to share a few stories about my adolescent experiences and why I thought a program like REAL was important for young folks. I related my stories to the four outward tenets of the program. I let them know that these concepts can be decisive in not only surviving as a male of color but also achieving as one. I disclosed to the boys that I was bringing REAL to them because I had learned the hard way and hopefully they would not have to. Not wanting to drown them in a lecture, I stopped there and moved on to a discussion of the student projects.

The high-school groups were interested in designing prints for T-shirts, making the booklet/CD, and putting together a video. I informed the boys that the program had limited financial resources, so projects would have to be a teamwork effort. Students asked where the T-shirts and CD were going to be sold and who was going to sell them. I replied that I would ask a few small neighborhood businesses to consign our products in their stores. I also asked the boys to think about people and places that they knew of that might be interested in selling our work.

Handing me his sketchbook was a junior named Juan DeLeon. Inside I found rather unique and imaginative drawings of lion heads, dragons, unicorns, and other mythological animals. Juan declared that he and his friends, sitting next to him, wanted to design T-shirts for the program. His classmate, Matthew Jackson, asked if he could write poetry for the booklet and CD. I responded to him and the rest of the group that they could contribute anything that they liked, but it had to be original and it had to be real. That is, it had to reflect their actual life and experiences. I wanted them to create a product that was an extension of who they were. In both the Monday and Thursday meetings, the hour we had was not long enough to answer all their questions about the projects. I let the boys know that we would finish up next week. Below are Matthew's and Jay's memories and first impressions of REAL's return in October 2000.

> **Matthew:** When other students told me about the REAL, I just thought it was another way for me to get out of class. If an opportunity comes up for you to get out of doing some work or hearing lectures, you're going to take them. When I got to REAL, we still had class discussions, but students had more freedom of speech. We were allowed to say anything that was on our minds dealing with school, teachers, or life. We could actually put in our info and that made me feel good. Plus the program was talking about some really cool stuff, as far as making music and a publication, and I wanted to be a part of that.
>
> **Jay:** I'll never forget the first meeting. Horace reintroduced himself and the ideas behind REAL. He pointed out that those are four qualities [respect, excellence, attitude, and leadership] that any person needs to succeed, whether it is in academics or the social aspects of life. He said that so many males are wrapped up in the streets, the hood, and trying to sur-

vive. It becomes a struggle, but there are so many meanings that the program's tenets can embody. He told us that the best way to be real was to become real in the sense of your thinking. The guys, who knew what Horace was talking about, had a look in their eyes saying, "You know what? He's right. This guy's telling the truth. He just basically summed up my neighborhood and my life in a way." His words made me want to stick around a whole lot more and contribute.

Even though Mel did not show up for either the Monday or Thursday session, he did attend Tuesday's middle-school meeting with Larry and me. Doris and Linda gave us the largest classroom on the first floor, and for good reason. The middle-school meetings were going to involve the participation of approximately thirty boys—one room overflowing with excited, preteen male energy.

From the very beginning of the meeting, a majority of the boys went back and forth joking around, teasing one another, going in and out of the room, and questioning why they had to be there. Larry, Mel, and I spent several minutes at the outset just trying to calm everybody down and get them to cooperate. After some effort, the room quieted enough to start the session, though some boys continued to goof off. We first asked students to introduce themselves and tell us their favorite school subject or hobby. All of the boys were either African American or Latino, varying in height, weight, shape, and skin tone. As dissimilar as their outward appearances were, so too were their interests and hobbies.

Soon after, we went over the program's tenets. The word "respect" was focused on heavily because of the continuing chatter and joking about that went on. We asked the boys to first define respect, then name people that they respected and why. Among all their responses, some characterized respect as doing what an older individual tells them to do. Others tied respect to fear. Many of the boys identified parents, grandparents, teachers, pastors, and police officers as people they respected because they had to.

I then brought up the importance of respect, particularly as it would relate to REAL. I told them that it was important for students to feel comfortable explaining their thoughts and opinions without being harassed by a classmate. I let them know that if REAL was going to be a special place for only them, then they needed to show respect for those persons in it. I think this struck a chord in them, something that clearly resonated, as even those who joked around finally quieted. Next, we went over excellence, attitude, and leadership. Linking each of these concepts with respect, we talked about how all four tenets are necessary in achieving one's goals in life. Larry made the point that accomplishing their different projects was going to require showing respect for everyone, putting forth excellence in their work, maintaining a positive attitude in carrying it out, and exemplifying leadership in helping others.

At that point, the boys excitedly discussed their ideas for T-shirt designs, videos, and the booklet/CD. As with the high-school students, I informed the middle-school students that the program's finances were slim and we would have to narrow down all their suggestions. One student, who had been dabbling at a computer for half the session, said that he and his classmates were learning website construction in their computer technology class. They offered to create a website for the program by branching it off the school's server. Using VCS's Internet provider would make the REAL website cost-free. The boys unanimously agreed that it was a good idea. In the coming months, all of the members of REAL were involved in designing prints for T-shirts, putting together the booklet/CD, documenting through video, and constructing the website.

After the session, Mel notified Larry and me that he was still working with the principal of Parma Elementary School and that he wanted us to join his efforts in bringing REAL there. I did not feel that it was a good idea for two reasons: (1) because of the damaging impression that we left upon one of the parents over the summer and (2) my hands were full from working with VCS. I told Mel that I wanted to concentrate my energy on VCS's boys and the different projects that they had in mind, especially as attendance was now looking promising. Larry also expressed that, because of time constraints with his job and family, he too could only focus on Visions.

After that conversation, Mel never returned to VCS as a REAL mentor. Despite his departure, we still communicated via Internet. Mel had decided to turn his full attention toward Parma Elementary. As for the money he collected for the REAL account, it was never distributed among mentors or students. And, as Visions was not financially supporting the program, all projects would be funded out-of-pocket—apparently my pocket.

By mid-November, I found students rushing to get to REAL meetings. A large majority of the boys could not wait to finish their writings or artwork and share them with the rest of the class. Middle-school sessions typically had thirty students. In the freshman and sophomore meetings, attendance averaged out to fifteen. The program also hosted all of the juniors, with a few regularly attending seniors. Apparently the seniors were involved with college preparatory activities that occurred during REAL's time slot, so their participation in REAL was limited. Nonetheless, the program hosted about half of the school's approximately sixty high-school boys.

To organize our space and meetings, students formed small clusters based on their projects. Student writing groups were actively engaged in creating hip hop lyrics and poetry and performing them in front of the class. I also brought in samples of songs to help explain the various elements that go to make them up (e.g., numerous tracks, instruments, and sound effects). Video crews from each class filmed our meetings as Larry and I supplied them with blank 8mm tapes and our video cameras. The middle- and high-school T-shirt design groups had come up with several samples for T-shirt prints. It had been agreed upon in previous sessions that, given our tight budget, members would sell REAL T-shirts to teachers, parents, and friends as a way to raise money for producing the CD and other student initiatives.

We then voted on one design for each program grouping (i.e., between the middle and high school). Juan DeLeon's surreal drawing of a lion's head, with the programs tenets arching over it, had been unanimously selected by his peers for the front of the T-shirt. For the back, Juan drew an exploding star with the program's acronym in the center. The students later proclaimed it the official REAL logotype. In the middle school, the work of Michael Hernandez, an eighth grader, was chosen. For the front of the shirt, Michael developed a cartoon figure of a man wearing a REAL T-shirt. For the back, all of his classmates elected Juan's logo. That week, I took the student prints to a printing company specializing in designing T-shirts and giving discounts.

Every other week over the next several months, meetings alternated between student arts-based activities and discussions and writings about their lives. We focused on violence as it exists in schools, in neighborhoods, in homes, in the world, how we learn it, how we perpetuate it, how we stop it, and the consequences if we do not. We engaged the young men in conflict resolution skits, asking them to come up with realistic strategies to resolve potentially violent situations. We discussed how news accounts and crime statistics inaccurately represented males of color, how these representations played on our own self-concepts, and what they as young people could do about it. We invited guest speakers to come in and talk about ways of breaking cycles of gang and domestic violence and beating the odds against them.

One guest speaker came in and discussed youth incarceration. His particular take on the subject came from his own personal experiences. His name was Martin Santiago. Like Larry, Martin was a fitness instructor and in his forties. He stood about 5'10", was well-built, and wore glasses that tempered his athletic veneer. Despite his outward appearance, Martin was soft-spoken with a calm and easy way about him. In his speech, he revealed how his adolescent years were filled with depression, drug and alcohol abuse, domestic violence, and criminal activities that eventually led to his incarceration. As Martin spoke, I thought about my own life and the lives of the VCS boys. While we may not have suffered the same kind of hardship as he had, our experiences indicated a shared struggle for acceptance, identity, understanding, and love. At the closing of each of his presentations, Martin was overwhelmed by applause and handshakes from students.

That following week, several of the middle-school boys asked if Martin was coming back to be a part of the program. Feeling the positive effect that he had on the students, I called Martin and told him about the student inquiries. I stated that, if he had the time, the program would enjoy having him on board as a mentor. I was not concerned about Martin's background. What struck me most was his sensitivity toward the boys and the way they connected with him. I notified him of the days and times that REAL met, and he stated that he would be open to working with the middle-school boys. That was more than fine with me. When I notified Doris and Linda about Martin's decision, they were delighted. They felt that it was important to have a Latino male, who was doing something positive with his life, working with young people of the same ethnicity.

Over the weeks leading up to the Christmas break, I contacted a nonprofit youth organization to partner with. It was called Sound Odyssey. Their mission was to help students create their own music CDs. Sound Odyssey was run by Jeff Warchowski, a local university music professor. He was interested in collaborating with REAL and asked for a small donation for his work with the program. As was the arrangement in Sound Odyssey's previous school projects, Jeff was to bring a portable studio into VCS. This would include a keyboard, microphones, and computerized audio engineering equipment. Doris and Linda said that they would provide a classroom after school where students could record their songs.

During the first week of December, Jeff made presentations to both the middle- and high-school boys. He first informed them that he believed anything could be music, whether it was a car horn, a rustling of leaves, a doorbell ringing, or water running. He then went over the elements of multi-tracking (e.g., beats, vocals, and background vocals) and voice inflection. He closed his talk by playing music composed and performed by high-school students from another charter school. Afterward, several students performed their poems and songs written for the REAL project. Jeff advised the students to have their work written and rehearsed prior to recording. And, on that note, VCS and REAL went on break for the Christmas holiday.

DIVERGENCE

VCS's spring semester started in the second week of January. Throughout that month, attendance in REAL meetings remained consistent. After school, Larry and I helped facilitate the making of a documentary by the middle- and high-school video teams. The short, unedited film showed candid footage of the performing arts aspect of program sessions. The boys performed self-written hip hop pieces and break-dance routines and recited poetry. They also conducted interviews with fellow REAL members asking them what the program meant to them. Their various perspectives indicated that REAL served as a way to learn more about their different arts-based projects, a space to talk about life issues with friends, a time to be away from teachers and schoolwork, and, for one student, a family-type of environment. At the time, I did not consider REAL to be a family, but from this young man's response, the program was something personal and intimate for him. I was glad that he felt that way and perchance so did others.

By the second week in March, VCS's third quarter was swiftly coming to a close. High-school students were scrambling around trying to make up last-minute classroom and homework assignments. Throughout this hectic week five, REAL high-school attendance dropped by nearly half. While some of the boys brought in their coursework to program sessions, others were working with teachers in their homerooms. During this time, students were less able to hand in their creative pieces as they had much less time to write them.

In a mad rush to make up their incomplete assignments, several of the high-school boys wanted to use their REAL artwork and writings as extra credit in their classes. As was agreed upon earlier, teachers were willing to accept student work from REAL as extra credit as long as it reflected what they were teaching. The high-school social studies teacher had no problem giving REAL members credit for their creative writing responses (e.g., hip hop pieces, narratives, and drawings) to the national tragedies occurring in Littleton, Colorado, and Santee, California. Regrettably, his coworkers were less amicable to such artistic expression as extra credit.

In an episode involving Matthew Jackson, he was failing his math class and his teacher did not see his poetry or hip hop writings as exactly related to algorithms or cosines. After she and I reached a compromise, I helped Matthew create spreadsheets and graphs that calculated and depicted REAL earnings from our T-shirts over a four-month period. She then passed him with a D.

Another episode was with Lee and Calvin. They were working on an essay assignment in their English class. It was not that their teacher could not see the connection between hip hop and English literature, but she wanted the boys to complete her specific assignment. So with that, I took Calvin and Lee after school to a university library where I often studied. We surfed the Internet for information on the topics of their essays. While they did most of the research, I assisted them with the semantics and syntax in their writing. After turning in their essays a few days later, the boys informed me that their teacher had given them an "Incomplete." When I asked her why, she stated that it was because I had assisted them. She maintained that since students were to do the assignment independently, it was unfair for Calvin and Lee to have my help. Not fully understanding her position and not wanting to make matters worse for Lee and Calvin, I didn't pursue the issue.

As REAL high-school attendance further declined, I knew this was no longer due to coursework or examinations. After experiencing a bit of friction with a few teachers regarding REAL as extra credit, I felt that something else was awry, but I couldn't quite put my finger on it. Later in the month of March, several students disclosed to me that their teachers were intentionally keeping them out of REAL. These boys claimed that teachers randomly kept a number of boys for Positive Living as they felt it was more important. Further inquiring about this matter, I asked student Matthew Jackson and VCS's computer technology teacher at the time, Tobias Stein.

> **Matthew:** From what I heard, Visions Charter School's Positive Living was in competition with REAL. Most of the teachers or the principals there may have thought that REAL didn't have any meaning because the school was based on the Positive Living principles. That's why they were probably keeping students. But REAL was different from Positive Living because REAL wasn't teaching us how to live a certain way, but the Positive Living was doing just that. To me, Positive Living was just common sense.
>
> **Tobias:** Visions had a much tightened discipline in fashion, in terms of dealing with their kids. And REAL gave them an outlet and an ability to vent their frustrations because they felt somewhat confined otherwise in the classrooms. However, teachers at Visions were under a lot of pressure to get a lot of stuff done. During our staff meetings, the big concern was the time to get everything done. REAL in the middle of the day began to interfere with what we needed to do for the administration. It was just so much going on at the time.

Since this entire venture had begun, I had been under the impression that REAL was established to help the VCS boys. From the number of male students involved with the program, it seemed to be doing just that. Maybe it was as Matthew stated, that the faculty felt REAL didn't have meaning. And perhaps it was competing with the school's Positive Living curriculum, though I didn't see it that way. I saw my efforts, along with Larry's, as a way to motivate the boys in and out of school.

In facing this obvious divergence from what I thought was a shared goal between REAL and Visions staff, I was reluctant to take the matter up with Doris or Linda for three reasons. One, it was hard to talk with them privately. They were constantly in meetings or on the telephone. Two, when I sought their financial assistance in late February for the making of the booklet/CD project, they jokingly brushed me off. Three, because of our lack of communication, I didn't know if they perceived the program as being beneficial the way that *they* wanted it to be. While REAL was attracting boys and involving them in constructive activities, it was not the magical cure for ceasing all of Doris and Linda's student discipline problems. And how could it be, especially when they and their staff had their own notions of how their boys should behave and perform?

Regardless of the declining teacher support, I believed that REAL was having a positive impact on the boys. I wasn't quite sure what the academic impact was, but I was certain that the program was reaching them affectively. I could see it in the way the middle- and high-school boys gravitated toward Martin, Larry, and me when we showed up at the school. These boys were genuinely excited about our presence and the activities planned for the day. Another indication that the program was reaching these young men was the piling-up of their telephone numbers on my desk. Many of the boys were always asking me to call them so that the REAL members could hang out after school, and we often did.

Student interactions with the mentors, both in and out of school, spoke to a need that was not being fulfilled in their daily lives. I believe that having the mentors around them was an extension of their desire to continue receiving the freedom, kinship, and positivity that the program brought. It was also their way of saying that REAL was cool and that they wanted more of it; they were getting something positive out of it. Just through our activities and discussions alone—it was positive. Contrary to what teachers may have felt about REAL, it was not trying to take anything away from VCS. Quite the opposite, it was striving to bring encouragement and motivation to the boys' schooling experience.

EMERGING REAL VOICES

By the end of March, there was good news. Third-quarter grades revealed that just over fifty percent of the boys, in both the middle and high school, had made the honor roll with a B average. A majority of the boys achieving this feat, and who had C and D averages in previous quarters, were regularly attending REAL members. In an interview with Doris, she attributed part of this student accomplishment to REAL. She stated that once the boys were in the program, they began to strive for achievement, and she linked this achievement with the brotherhood that the program fostered. Linda also commended the program's efforts, asserting that the mentors put the boys in a position of leadership, which in turn gave them voice and empowerment. During that school year, Lisa Delgado was the school's office manager. She gives her impression of the program at VCS:

> At Visions, I could see that REAL made a difference with the boys because originally they were not focused on school or schoolwork. They were more into sports and playing around. They weren't serious about their studies, their homework, or their testing. After REAL got there and started working with the kids, I saw a gradual turnaround in the way they behaved toward the girls, themselves, and adults. Then, we started seeing more boys get on the honor roll and get better grades on their report cards. The kids started doing their work and doing what they had to do and taking responsibility for what they did wrong and what they didn't do.

Although a few teachers continued to hold onto their male students for Positive Living, attendance did not diminish any further. Freshman and sophomore groups leveled off at about ten to twelve boys per session. The juniors remained consistent, with the exception of two who were nonattending. Three seniors, heavily involved with VCS's college preparation course, attended program meetings off and on.

April marked the beginning of audio recordings for the REAL Voices CD. Every Friday after school, Jeff showed up with his audio equipment. Sessions were held for two hours in a sixth-grade classroom on the first floor. Even though the booklet was to precede the CD, I had only received a few writings from various students. However, in recording sessions, the boys brought in their pieces and recorded them. They performed poems, skits, songs, and comedy sketches—all of which were original. Even though I appreciated their enthusiastic participation, none of the boys was well-rehearsed. As a result, multiple retakes ran our sessions overtime. In fact, the initial five weeks that I thought recording the CD would take turned into months, extending well into the summer.

The first full week in June marked the program's final sessions. We threw class parties, with chips and drinks, for both the middle- and high-school sessions. These final sessions also invited the boys to openly reflect on their last eight months in the program. From every grade, the boys suggested ways of improving REAL. Their ideas included creating more T-shirts, having more field trips, spending less time talking about social and political issues and more time on art activities, creating REAL hats and scarves, having a REAL bus to drive students around, painting a mural, having a fund-raiser, putting more money into the program, and making no change at all.

Since the REAL meetings with the juniors had consistently high turnouts, I asked them to write a few sentences about if and/or why REAL should return for the next school year. I informed them that I was going to give their statements to Doris and Linda as a part of an overall program evaluation. Written student responses included: members liked utilizing their arts-based skills in program projects; they enjoyed bonding with me and their peers; the program helped their studies by giving them a more positive attitude; REAL was motivational; students had the opportunity to express their feelings; it broadened their idea about what being a man means (e.g., responsibilities, vulnerabilities, expectations); and it helped students discover the meaning of brotherhood. Paris Brandy, the elected president of REAL in its pilot run, wrote down what ultimately became the program's motto: "REAL is a medium of expression for the previously unexpressed."

By mid-June, VCS's school year was finishing up as fourth-quarter grades were being released. Similar to the previous quarter, male students made up approximately 50 percent of the honor roll. A majority of those boys were in REAL. Once again, Doris and Linda had correlated this increase with the assistance from the mentors. Despite their attributing this accomplishment to us, raising student grades was not our primary focus. Larry, Martin, and I believed that what we did in the program was not solely about positively impacting student academics but was also about elevating the mind-sets and emotional states of young people.

Bringing REAL to students meant asking them to look within themselves and make constructive changes in their own lives, whether academically, socially, mentally, or spiritually. It meant helping them build self-esteem and self-concept by using problem-solving activities, having discussions about their identity, addressing their needs and concerns, and helping them work through their personal problems. With that as a foundation, the boys could then develop a greater appreciation for school and the long-term goals that it purports.

For me, the truest accomplishment was developing relationships with these young people. It was helping them nurture their lives as boys growing into men. While VCS's primary concern was how the boys related to teachers and to education, REAL was also interested in how the boys felt about their peers, their family, their neighbors, their communities, their world, and themselves. We wanted them to know that despite the skewed images and negative perceptions that they faced on a daily basis, there was someone who wanted to understand them and see them as young men growing and changing, needing and wanting. It was important for them to see and know individuals, outside of their teachers, who cared and desired to give back to them. As Martin Santiago put it, "REAL was about taking time to take time." And we did so by reaching out with love as often as we could.

EPILOGUE

At the end of VCS's school year, several of the REAL boys continued to work on their contribution to the CD. One of the summer sessions was held at Jeff's recording studio located on his university's west town campus. Other tapings were engineered by one of Jeff's colleagues, Frank Delgado. Frank had a mini recording studio situated in the back of his apartment. Calvin, Jay, Matthew, Lee, and I went there twice a week for three-hour recording sessions.

By the end of June, the CD was finished, or so I thought. To my surprise, Matthew had been creating his own recording studio in his bedroom. Using audio engineering software and some piecemeal audio equipment (sound mixer, stereo receiver, equalizer, and two microphones), Matthew had replicated the technical layout that he had observed working with Jeff and Frank. With his "industrial space" as he called it, Matthew suggested that we could add additional songs to the REAL CD. Loving to rap and be in the studio, Jay, Lee, and Calvin were all for the idea. Every Saturday afternoon I picked up the boys and we made our way to Matthew's house where we often stayed until late evening hours.

In the last week of July, the CD was finally complete and the boys were satisfied with their finished product. The master recording was then taken to a CD copying company where one hundred duplicates were made. As for the booklet (originally planned to come before the CD), the boys decided to scale down cost by designing an inlay to fit inside the CD jewel case. For the beginning of the new school year, "REAL Voices: Original Beats, Rhythms, and Rhymes" was ready to be marketed. Initially, copies were sold to the schoolmates and friends of program members for $7. In the months to follow, I took the liberty of marketing the CD for $10 at conferences and other speaking engagements. The money earned from sales was put into a savings account and used for future REAL projects and student outings.

Hanging out with the boys during the summer months also afforded me the opportunity to develop stronger ties with their parents. I was invited to different family gatherings (e.g., birthdays and summer barbecues), where I began to feel like an uncle or a cousin. Whenever there was a personal issue with the boys, their parents often phoned me to speak about it. Additionally, I often served as a helping hand with their son in cases where they needed to be taken to the dentist, the library, a job interview, and, in one instance, to traffic court. As a part of being an effective mentor for these young men, it was important to have the approval and confidence of their parents. In one instance, Calvin's mother told me that it was good having me around to help keep her son out of trouble. Although Calvin's father was very much a part of his life, she stated that Calvin still needed additional male support.

Matthew's father also appreciated the time that I took with his son. He commented:

> Parents have to work every day. A parent comes home and talks with their kids for a short time and then the next thing you know that parent is asleep from the long work day. Mr. Hall was like auxiliary backup. He came in and helped with what the parents lacked in doing at that time. That's really needed because some kids don't really feel that they should come to their parents when their parents are really tired. They don't want to put their problems on the parent because they feel that the parents have enough problems on their own.

In early September I called Doris to see if REAL was going to be reinstated as an in-school program. In our phone conversation, Doris informed me that the program could no longer use their Positive Living time slot. If it was going to return, it had to be rescheduled for after school. I reminded her of the problems associated with that time. She responded by saying that her staff believed that the boys attending REAL were missing out on Positive Living activities—something that the school wanted to heavily promote for the new academic year. As it turned out, the teachers decided to keep *all* of their boys during that time.

Even though I had suspected this growing teacher sentiment months before, I felt that the stimulating effects that the program provided was enough to keep REAL fixed during the day. Obviously, I was wrong. Respecting Doris's decision, I made no argument. Instead, I remained optimistic that the boys would continue to attend sessions despite the after-school time slot. With this hope in mind, I agreed to run REAL after school. Doris then told me that the newly hired after-school coordinator would call me to discuss the formalities of bringing the program back. Days would turn into months before I received any such phone call.

Eventually that year, Larry, Martin, and I went on to work with the VCS boys after school, despite our low student turnout. In the months to follow, I networked with a host of teachers and principals and was able to expand REAL to other city schools. Larry and Martin remained consistent mentors, assisting me in program functions. I was even able to acquire the help of a female adult mentor in creating an all-girls group for program meetings. As for Calvin, Jay, Matthew, and Lee, the boys worked on another album entitled, "REAL Voices Vol. 2: Misperceptions." Three of the boys currently attend out-of-state universities and one works in the city.

I have learned a great deal from this entire mentoring experience. I realize that, as educators and school administrators, before we can develop programs and curriculum to "assist" young people, there must first be an understanding and empathy for what students are experiencing on an everyday basis. A way to discover how students are feeling and living is to provide them with someone trusting to talk to and a safe space to do it in. It is in this space that they can, individually or collectively, think, explore, and organize constructive, as well as realistic, ways for dealing with their problems. REAL offered this space.

By providing children and adolescents with a chance to speak, we are afforded a rare opportunity to know them in all their fullness. In moments of their voice, we are able to hear their dreams, visions, goals, fears, and anxieties. Knowing these things means that we have taken the time to talk to our young people and are discovering ways of reaching them. It also means learning to accept them unconditionally, seeing them as humans and as individuals who, like all of us, need love, care, hope, friendship, and an understanding of who we are in the world around us.

7

REAL Profiles: Mentors and Mentees

This final chapter presents commentary from REAL mentors and mentees. Pseudonyms are used in the interest of confidentiality.

LARRY SKYLAR

Larry Skylar is forty-two years old and has been married for seven years. With assistance from his wife, Larry financially supports their three children as a personal trainer. He says that his business is "self-sufficient," not locking him into any one particular gym. Instead, he utilizes different health clubs, renting space for himself and his clients. Larry describes himself as "a father who is always striving to provide the best for his family."

Larry attended his first REAL session in the first summer, during the program's car wash venture. At the beginning of that session, Larry introduced himself and briefly went over his background. He informed the boys that he joined REAL as a way to give back to his community by serving as a role model for youth. He went on to add that the words respect, excellence, attitude, and leadership were a "blueprint for life." He stated how each word is essential for building healthy relationships and growing into manhood.

In Visions Charter School's 2000–2001 academic year, Larry stayed with the program, volunteering as a mentor for the middle-school boys. In his time with REAL, he and I developed a strong friendship. Much of what he says in the following interview comes out of the program's first full year at VCS.

*In REAL, I served as a mentor and a facilitator of meetings. My partici-
pation was on and off again to some degree because of my family and job
commitments. I was mainly there for classroom sessions and didn't have
the time to participate in some of the outings or get-togethers that the other
mentors were able to do. My busy life affected what could have been close
relationships with the kids. I would love to win the lottery and not have to
work, so I could spend all my time with my kids as well as mentoring other
kids.*

*To me, mentoring is enlightening and encouraging young people. It's
being there to answer their questions, to give them a pat on the back, to
show them that there's a wider world out there and the ways that they can
be a part of that world. I think that so many of these kids today lack vision.
They can't see past their block, their hood, city, or whatever it is. So they
need to be exposed to as much as possible and then maybe something will
click. As a mentor, I want to continue to show them how they can be a part
of this world and encourage them to make that transformation happen.*

*Being involved with REAL gave me an opportunity to reach out to kids
and make a difference in some small way. Malcolm X once said that you're
either part of the problem or part of the solution, and there's obviously a
real big problem out there. Some of us can be big parts of the solution and
paint in broad strokes, while some us have to fill in the dots. Maybe some-
day I can paint a broader stroke. REAL was at least a way for me to get
involved with the community and fill in some of those dots, making an
effort to change things in a positive way.*

*For the most part, I worked with the middle-school boys at Visions. I
think REAL was very effective because you saw those lights popping on in
their heads when we were talking with them. They were jumping up,
wanting to speak, wanting to contribute. The curriculum aroused them
and was good at getting their opinion. They responded a lot. I could see
them actually think things out and come up with original thoughts about
things outside their box. We did conflict resolution skits and showed them
certain ways of handling and conducting themselves in school and out of
school. I certainly saw a lot of kids change over the school year and become
more confident in just the way they carried themselves. It's the knowledge*

that empowers them. What little knowledge we were able to impart with them, asking them to think about it and examine it, I think made a huge difference.

Outside of role-playing skits, we also brought in guest speakers. I think that's very important. That's something that I would like to see done on a more regular basis. Guest speakers can be very effective. With us seeing students on a regular basis, the familiarity won't be the same. You create a little bit of a wild factor. Whether that wild factor has to be a celebrity, I don't know necessarily, but someone who can bring something different to the table than the regular mentors. That person could be a celebrity, someone successful, or someone just trying to make a difference, but it should be someone students can relate to. Students need to see that person and say, "Wow, if he or she did it, maybe I can do it too. Maybe I can make a difference politically or culturally." They need to hear from someone who has maybe made a whole lot of money, is successful in making a business, and has come to tell their story of about why they're successful. Guest speakers have to tell kids why and how they can do it too.

I've always considered REAL to be a blueprint for success. The first thing in any blueprint is a foundation. If you don't have that, you don't have anything. The foundation that we give kids is an understanding of how to get over in the world. You get over by understanding what's going on in the world around you. You have to be aware of things. The things that we talk about in REAL are the things going on today, its different meanings, and how it all impacts us; for example, what's going in Iraq, Iran, and the global market and how do those things impact us here.

REAL is also a blueprint in the sense that you have to have a plan and a direction. It's hard to stay pat in life today. You're either moving forward or you're going backwards. And if you're starting out three steps behind, then it's even more important that you are constantly moving forward and in the right direction. This is hard to do if you don't know which way to go or how to get there. Worse yet, you might not know that the choice exists. REAL is a blueprint because we break it down and say that not only is this a reachable goal or destination, but here's how you can do it and how to get there besides saying you need to study and do good in school.

Don't get me wrong. School is important, but it's not the be-all and end-all that it once was. Our academic system is seriously flawed. It's not necessarily turning out thinkers, doers, and wanters. It's kind of just turning out drones, especially most of the public schools. We need to teach kids to be other than that. REAL informs students that school is one of the ways to get over. We let them know that it's part of the blueprint and that they can get something out of it. But outside of what they learn in school, we also teach them other ways to define success for themselves.

When these students hear successful men telling them how to deal with school and their world, they really listen and open up to us. And I think that's important because, from what I've experienced, kids often need someone to talk to about their lives. We serve as a bridge between students and teachers or students and the school. There's always going to be that static between kids and teachers and that struggle against authority. REAL kind of straddles that fence to serve as an advocate for kids. For instance, we tell them that whatever they feel about their teachers, they have to use them to their advantage. Anything else and they're just wasting time, treading water, or getting washed downstream.

On the other hand, teachers, when they're frustrated with a student, might not know that kid's situation as well as we do because the kid hasn't opened up to them. Sometimes there are walls that exist between students and teachers, when they're not from the same background or culture as most of the kids. Just as kids see the world as this great enigma, I think it works the other way too. A lot of teachers who have come up in different backgrounds have no idea or concept of what these kids are going through in their lives. They don't look behind the curtain because what's behind there can be so shocking at times that you just want to sweep it under the carpet and move on, but you can't until you understand it. You have to understand what's going on and what kids are dealing with on a day-to-day basis, which might make them act out or hard to reach. As mentors, we're able to inform the teacher and advocate for the student. This can make their job easier and give them a greater understanding of the students. We are there to help teachers, not supersede them, and that whole political thing. We want to inform teachers who are wondering what's going on with their students. More information may make it easier to reach those kids.

My experience with REAL has reinforced the idea that everyone can do something to help turn a kid's life around or change the direction they're going in. You can be important to a kid in that way. It's something that should be done at whatever level you can do it at. I think that's something that people should take into consideration, especially if wanting to help young Black men. There's such a catastrophic problem that we have out there with them. And I don't think anybody else can really fix it but other Black men. But helping out can be tough when you're trying to get your life together and handle responsibilities like your own kids. Still, I have to remember that those other kids are my kids too. That's what I always felt in the back of my mind. If I didn't make some kind of effort to help those kids, I wouldn't exactly know how to help my own.

I think REAL is a very positive program. I'd love to see it grow. I'd love to see it become an institution. I'd love to be more a part of it in some way or another. I definitely see it as being one of those answers to the solution of the big problem that kids are facing. And that problem is not getting any smaller. There's not going to be one big blanket answer. There needs to be these small answers from city to city, town to town, community to community. No one's going to write a big check. Even if they did, it wouldn't help the total problem. You have to change minds. More importantly, you have to change mind-sets, and that's what REAL does.

MARTIN SANTIAGO

Martin Santiago, age forty-two, is one of the program's first regularly involved mentors. Martin earned his general education diploma in Joliet's correctional facility and took some college courses through correspondence. He is currently self-employed as a physical fitness professional. Martin says that he has a sincere desire to help children and is always striving to make a positive impact on them. His message to kids: "No matter what your circumstances are, no matter how difficult it is, if you really want to, you can change your life." Martin asserts that his ultimate life goal is to find truth and meaning by taking up his cross and following in the footsteps of Jesus Christ.

When I first joined REAL, I saw a lot of great things happening with it. I've seen a lot of programs and I've been to a lot of schools, and REAL was a program that I felt really inspired kids. I wanted to be a part of that simply because I know that kids need a role model, a mentor, or a friend. It's amazing how many are out there with that hunger for someone to care about them, to listen to them, to mentor them, to teach them, and to set limits for them.

For me, mentoring has been a way of repairing some of the wrongs that I committed as a juvenile. In my younger years, I know I hurt people. Mentoring became a way for me to somehow give back and make reparations. A friend of mine said that it's easy to just write a check, but the person who goes and actually makes the sacrifice and spends the time is the one who really makes the impact. It's just my way of trying to give back and not just talk about how nice it would be but to actually do it. I would challenge more people to take up their cross and do it.

In REAL, I see myself as a guy who can come into meetings and connect with children heart to heart, showing them that I respect and care for them. My disposition helps create the atmosphere where they can open up and talk. We get them thinking and discussing and questioning and arguing in a constructive way—just giving them some expression of freedom, even if it is the old Socratic method of questioning.

Being a part of the program, from my point of view, has allowed me to be hands-on in a classroom. That's the experience that I found most fulfilling with the program—being there with them, listening to their stories, hearing about their challenges and day-to-day struggles to make it. As mentors, we don't offer them all the answers, but the fact that we sit there and listen to them, even if it is for five minutes, is needed. Sometimes, a student will pull one of the mentors off into a corner because they had something to say and they know we're there to listen. So besides reading out loud and having discussions about current world events, we are also there for a little sidebar.

Another part of what we do in the program is inform students about their options and what the world is really like out there. We try to portray what's really happening. I can remember one of our role-playing skits where we put kids in a situation of being stopped by the police. We showed them their options and asked them to choose the best alternative. Everyone had fun doing it. At one point, they were all laughing at each other. But everybody, including the mentors, went away understanding exactly what the message was for the day. The message was reality. We show kids realistic alternatives in certain situations. That's our biggest message.

The thing that I enjoy most about being in the REAL Youth Program is building relationships with children, parents, and the other mentors. For kids, it's important to give them a sense of belonging, especially the toughest ones. Those are the ones often hanging on the edge. We always try to create classrooms that are caring, respectful, and safe. When kids sense that you care about them and that you respect them, they begin to feel more secure. By shutting our mouths and listening to their feelings, they realize that we respect and care for them. And because REAL is not a part of the school staff, students can open up and say things to us without fearing that we'll tell their teacher or principal. In this way, we serve as a refuge for students, providing a comfort level to teach them, advise them, caution them, and offer them the opportunities that are out there.

In some of the schools that we've worked at, the surrounding streets and communities aren't always safe. There's a lot of crime and the kids know it. Inside the school, there's also violence. Unfortunately, it seems to be a part of the social fabric and it affects children. In REAL, the mentors try to address that in the classroom. We talk about violence, the damage it causes, and the abuse that it brings. Some of the kids that we've worked with experience violence and abuse every day. We try to explain why violence doesn't always work and how in the long run they're better off finding a more intelligent way of dealing with it, in a way that it doesn't turn around and hurt them like violence does.

The other aspect of showing that we, as mentors, care for a child is by talking about our experiences that we've had in the past. We share that wisdom with them. We open up to them and show them that we can be vulnerable in front of them. They poke fun at us sometimes, but in the long run it creates an open forum—a part of the formula that REAL uses. When we finally end our program at a school, sometimes kids will walk up and give me a painting, a drawing, a poem, or a letter saying that I'll miss you or thank you for listening. That brightens up my day every time.

As for building relationships with parents, it's important to meet and talk with them. One day, at the end of a session, I met one of the students' moms. I congratulated her on such a polite and intelligent young man that she had brought up. I told her that he's a pleasure to work with and that she deserved a lot of credit as a parent. I stopped there, but I just felt very strongly about that. Here's a parent that shows up, who's there asking questions, and you don't see much of that. That involvement makes a world of difference. If a lot more of these young people had that, it's my guess that we would probably see a lot less crime. We would probably see a lot less teen pregnancy and a reduction in a lot of the problems that our young people are facing. Because of a lack of family support, an overall level of stress in young people's lives today has quadrupled.

In terms of having friendships with the REAL mentors, it's important. I have a certain level of respect for each one because they're there for the same reason that I'm there. No matter what their background or how they make their livelihood, they've taken time out of their day to show up for these kids. I think that brings on an automatic bond between us, and the kids see that; they sense it. I remember the kids making me laugh when they asked if the REAL mentors were together all of the time. They pictured us going everywhere together.

It's also important for mentors to have a workable relationship between teachers and administrators. It's really refreshing to come into a school, meet with the school staff, and get their support. That's what benefits everyone in the long run. We've had examples of schools that brought us in but didn't promote the program. The kids didn't know if we were there or not, and the staff didn't know either. That's the discouraging part. If an administrator wants to see results, as they often do, then they need to communicate and show their support for programs like REAL. The immediate results may not be high test scores or good grades, but if a child's life has improved emotionally or that child has realized that he has options in

life, can you really measure that? I see results as students going back to
class or anywhere in their daily life and doing better in whatever they do.
Everything stems from a sense of self-respect, respect for others, and a good
attitude. I think those are the things that will improve a school in general.
*   Twenty-five years ago, I thought success was something totally different.*
I envisioned success as me strolling through the grounds of a huge mansion
and having all this money, jewelry, and material wealth. Now at forty-
two, many, many years later and having gone through many, many expe-
riences, I realize what's important. In my opinion, it is helping your fellow
man. In my case, it's children because they're very dear to my heart; they
are the future. They're the ones we're handing the reins over to and they
are in trouble. God help us if we don't make a change from what we see
these days in the news and media. We need to get to work. We really do.
That means individually and collectively. Myself, I'm mentoring, public
speaking, finishing my book, and being a voice for youth. It's very easy to
kind of fade into the background and live your own life, thinking things
will take care of themselves. As adults, we've done too much of that and
now we're paying the consequences for it. I think we're all involved and
should be held accountable. If we keep our silence and do nothing, then I
think we're all accountable for our collective misfortunes. We're a society;
we're a community and our children are important. I don't think we see
that. And if there's any way that I can help people see that, then I will
have done my duty.

CALVIN JOHNSON

Calvin Johnson is eighteen years old. His hobbies include photography,
writing, and watching movies that he says "make you think." Calvin
describes himself as funny, intelligent, and critical. He lives with his
mother and father in a two-flat located on the far south side of Chicago.
His mom is a nurse holding an associate's degree. He feels that he can
talk to her about anything. Calvin's father attended one year of college
and then stopped. He says he finds it difficult to talk with his father,
especially when his dad is heavily intoxicated. Calvin has one brother
and two sisters; one is a half sister. His brother lives in another state,

and his half sister resides on the west side of town. He describes his relationship with them as "distant." Being that he has more contact with his older sister, he feels closest with her. She is currently working on her bachelor's degree. Calvin stated that his neighborhood lacks positive things for him to do, so he often travels to downtown Chicago, where he listens to open mic poetry and buys CDs. Calvin attended Visions Charter School from the fall of 1998 to the spring of 2003. During his last two years there, he was an honor roll student, and he has been a participant in the REAL Youth Program for approximately three years. Although he has been involved with several other youth programs, he claims that he finds stronger bonds of brotherhood within REAL.

I've been in the REAL Youth Program since 2000—three years. I thought REAL was dope because it gave us the chance to take time out of Positive Living, where we weren't really doing anything. Positive Living is a class at Visions where we just sit down and talk about issues. That's what it was like in the beginning, and then it slowly turned into a study hall. We could talk in study hall, but we couldn't talk like we can in REAL. REAL gave us the chance to really talk. It was a bunch of boys and no teacher. Well, Mr. Hall was the teacher, but not like the other kind of teacher, so we could be more real.

When I first got involved with REAL, it was because teachers said they would give us a credit for history or something for attending. But then the more I got involved, I really started liking the program. I don't think they ever did give us credit. If they did, they gave credit to the Positive Living class.

When I first joined REAL, the other guy [Mel Jackson] was more business-like. It was about doing car washes and making some money. But when Mr. Hall took over, it became "We gonna read some books and learn some stuff, or we gonna make a CD and learn some stuff, or we gonna kick it to these restaurants and talk." That attracted me to the program. It became more of a brotherhood and I learned a lot. I learned you gotta be a leader sometimes. You gotta be who you are and when you say something, do it. I also learned that it's good to have people who you can call;

people you can call at night if something happened and you need to get it off your chest. Sometimes you can't talk to your parents. It's good to have another adult figure that you can call and tell them your issues, your problems.

Last summer when I was walking down the street from a party, a guy had a gun. He was like "Don't walk on this side of the street." What else could I do? I mean, I had to do what he said; he had a gun. Afterwards, I called Mr. Hall. I told him what happened, so that I wouldn't go out and do something that might get me killed. Talking to him helped because I was able to think things through.

Another thing that attracted me to the program was Mr. Hall's charisma. When he'd come up to the school, everyone was like, "Mr. Hall! Mr. Hall!" He's positive, and that's cool because you don't get too many older males who are like that. Some people you see, they're not really men yet. They ain't really got that mentality. Mr. Hall showed the younger kids how to be by just being there. He's someone to talk to and get inspired by and get motivated to know that you can do it, to know that you can succeed.

Most of my classes also made me want to go to REAL. When I was in class, I wasn't doing so well; it was kind of stressing me out a lot. So I knew that if I went to REAL, everything would be okay. I just needed some relax time. I needed to feel comfortable. It was like a brotherhood. You could come there, talk about something, and it just relaxed you. It made your day better. You felt more positive.

REAL was helpful because it gave me a break. It was more effective than the lunch break because you got a chance to talk. I guess me coming from a dysfunctional family I needed an outlet. I needed to tell somebody that I came from a dysfunctional family. Instead of keep telling myself, I needed to get it off my chest. By being around a bunch of your friends that gets it off your chest and, indirectly, by being able to hang around. I liked that we all got to hang out and that we all could go bowling and have fun. It wasn't a curriculum like, "Do this here! Write this paper! Read this book!" But we still learned things, so that's cool.

Now one of the best things about REAL is that you can curse sometimes, *as long as you're not like, "F*ck you!! F*ck you!" or all that. And I think a lot of teachers don't really see that. They consider that not to be realistic, but in reality teenagers curse all the time—that's mainly what we do. You're in a cool place when you can do that. REAL is like you're in school but you're not really in school, but you are in school and that's cool. REAL means being yourself around people who are cool and who are being themselves too.*

If I had to make changes to the program it would be to have more of it. At Visions, REAL became an after-school program and people just wanted to go home. And then it started coming every other week. REAL needed more consistency. I would also have more events like bowling, going to the movies, making more T-shirts, and taking pictures of stuff. REAL should also expand to more schools, go on trips, speak at big universities, and go to college fairs. The spirit of the youth needs that. They need to be doing positive stuff. I really wouldn't make any other changes because not too many programs would meet with me on a Saturday or help me go out and find a job. Not too many programs would do that.

REAL is extremely important to me. It's a supplement to your mentality. It's like here take this vitamin, take this vitamin, take this vitamin. It just helps you grow. I think like a lot of people already have "REAL," but not like REAL. They have "REAL" with their peers and with somebody who might be older in the group, but it's not as positive; it's just negative. We go on the block and it's a bunch of people. They're having "REAL"; they're talking about real stuff, but they're not going to schools talking about positive stuff that will affect their life. And I think that is really needed.

Sometimes when you're in REAL, you think you don't need it. But when you don't go to REAL, you're like, "Man, I need REAL." Programs like REAL are important for males and females. It's something about an older male teaching kids—you learn hands-on.

LEE CAMACHO

Lee Camacho is nineteen years old. His hobbies include reading, writing, and emceeing. He says, "I pretty much do anything that's interesting to me." He describes himself as an "open-minded, intelligent, sophisticated being." He adds, "I feel that I've grown from being ignorant and uncontrollable to actually a more subtle, mellow, and understanding person."

I was in the ninth grade when I first started regularly attending REAL. When the program came to me, I was actually failing in school. It was terrible. I couldn't maintain a D average. I was slacking off. Then, this guy named Horace Hall came in and sat down with various youth and explained the program. He said something like, "You can take advantage of this, if you want to. If you don't want to, it's cool. I can vibe with you. I go through the same things you go through daily." Mr. Hall seemed concerned about us. He personally said to me, "These are the grades you have. This is what I can help you get. It's up to you though. I can only show you the door; you have to walk through it."

Unfortunately, at the time, I didn't utilize REAL in the aspect of actually earning a higher grade point average. Instead, I used it as a way to get out of class because I found it to be very entertaining, more than my regular classes. The discussions were informative. I was given information on stuff like stereotypes, generalizations, and things of that nature. It opened my eyes to things in society that aren't what you think they are. In our discussions, Mr. Hall wasn't someone talking at you, but someone talking with you, who could actually feel the vibe that you had. He blended with the youth. He was cool and on the students' level. He wasn't like, "I'm not on your level, so sit down and chill with your friends." He was more like, "If you want to sit down and talk with me about your problems, come talk to me. I can help you out, if you want my help." It was inspirational. REAL was like a savior because we bonded with someone who opened up to us and helped us understand our feelings.

I found in our group meetings that I'm not the only one that has certain issues or ideas. Many of my fellow classmates had the exact same opinions, and we felt strongly about them. I felt like my classmates were on my level, and I could share something personal with them because they probably experienced or went through the same things that I had. I felt we could actually talk with each other about certain issues that were private or just

*guys bonding. A brotherhood is what I would call it. In REAL, I got to be
myself, my actual self. I didn't have to portray anything that wasn't me. I
felt that, whatever I was doing or participating in, I was giving my 100
percent and there was no sugarcoating it. If you were in REAL, you could
be yourself, while being respectful. I could portray my image the way I
wanted myself to be.*

*I eventually started wanting to have REAL more than once a week. It's
like REAL became addictive. It's kind of like having a sweet tooth and
somebody gives you a little piece of a candy bar, but you want the whole
thing. You want more of REAL, but you're only going to get as much as
they give you. It actually got to the point where one day Mr. Hall wasn't
there and REAL was cancelled. But the students had a meeting anyway.
We all took our class break and had a REAL session. Students were electing
to be the moderator so we could have the meeting. It's funny because people came from other classrooms, even those not in the program, to check
out our session.*

*For me, REAL became the gang in my neighborhood that I joined a
long time ago, but with more positive views. I feel that REAL should be
everywhere. It serves as a mentoring program for youth. If REAL was
global, you probably wouldn't even see gangs in the street. But if they were
gangs, they'd be REAL gangs. We'd pass out flyers, instead of spray painting graffiti. REAL is real and it's awesome.*

*The mentors in REAL are cool too. They're not kids, but you can see
the kids inside of them. They want to reach out to the youth in the program. They'll do anything as long as they can make an impact on your
life, as long as they can make you change something that's negative into
positive. Their support is excellent. It's male support. I've got female support from my mother, but I never really had a male mentor during high
school when there were a lot of distractions. I haven't had a father figure
in my life, so I guess you can say that the mentors kind of serve as the
childhood fathers that I've never had. They're actually good role models,
inspiring me to do positive things and that's pretty cool.*

*Mentoring from my point of view is not really instructing a person, but
making an impact on someone you know that needs motivation or some-*

one you know that has the potential but won't realize it until you actually make it clear to them. Mentoring is serving as a role model for that person. Everyone needs a role model no matter how intelligent or sophisticated they are. They need someone like a mentor so that they can have something positive in their lives.

I have multiple mentors. I have Horace Hall, Cedrick Mack [another REAL mentor], and my uncle, Lenny. They aren't childhood mentors either. These are adults that I can actually bond with, who are more on my level and that I feel I can talk to; they can relate to me. Even though they are adults, I feel like we all go through some of the same things in life. Though those things might be introduced to them on a higher level because they're older, I still feel like I'm them and they're me. They're whole vibe is "I'm not going to let you fail," and I admire that.

Before I got into REAL, I felt more or less like just another African American stereotype. But REAL has actually changed my thinking into living outside the box. I feel like I can achieve and accomplish a lot. I never thought I had it, but my mentors served as an inspiration. REAL encourages me to do more things in life before my time is up. It has inspired me to actually succeed and reach for more. I've realized that REAL actually tried to help me back then. I didn't really take advantage of it, but now I see that REAL has made me a better person, and I feel that I can do not only 100 percent but 200 percent in anything that I want to accomplish. Basically, REAL is a gateway. It has helped me realize my potential and things I can accomplish.

JERMAINE CARTER

Jermaine Carter is nineteen years old. He is light brown in complexion, tall, and hefty. Jermaine is a 2002 graduate of VCS. His extracurricular activities while at Visions were REAL and the basketball team. Currently, Jermaine is enrolled as a freshman at a four-year college in southern California. He says that he wants to own his own business and has decided to choose business administration as his college major. Jermaine firmly believes that he has to set goals and reach for them because of what the ill past has taught him. He has one sister who is currently attending VCS as a freshman. When not at college, Jermaine stays with his mother in an apartment complex on the far south side of Chicago. His mother is a kindergarten teacher for the Chicago public school system. His stepfather died in 1999.

In March of 2001 at VCS, I asked the junior class members of REAL to write a few words to the school's directors on how they felt about the program and if it should return for the following school year. Since I had the most success with this class, I felt their responses would influence Doris and Linda to bring REAL back for the next academic year. Student responses were incorporated into a four-page document that summarized program agenda, curriculum, and potential projects.

All of the boys expressed a fondness for me and the program as well as their need for it to return. I greatly appreciated their words. However, I found Jermaine's response to be one of the more heartwarming and compelling of the student writings. In all the time that followed, I never forgot his words. For this research, I wanted him to say more about his situation at that time and what REAL meant to him.

I never really had a father figure in my life. I had a stepfather when I was at a young age like fifteen or sixteen. When he died, I didn't really know which road to take. Should I keep going or should I just drop out? For me, dropping out was really about being in school. In school, everyone is rated from the smartest to the dumbest. So if you don't really get anything, you just feel kind of dumb, but you're really not. You just need another way to look at things, to see really them. You can get anything you want to.

But I guess that's how I was feeling and I just wanted to drop out. Sometimes females get pregnant and drop out. Sometimes people have family problems at home or they're not concentrating in school. Whatever it is, it's always a problem. I think that with most teenagers today there's a lot of outside things that don't focus students on school. There's a lot of gangs and different things like that. So it's all about you and what's going on with you at the time. You just have to keep that focus to keep going to school because if not, you're just going to drop out and feel like you're hopeless, like you don't have anything.

That's kind of where REAL came in for me. Two of my hardest subjects were math and biology. And I remember REAL used to meet every Thursday. At the time, I was feeling kind of stressed out because I didn't know what to do. I wasn't getting help in my classes or at least I wasn't putting forth that effort to get help. But when I got to REAL, I started realizing. We'd had conversations about different topics like the criminal justice system, the violence in California, how to budget your money, going to college, and different other things like that. Those were all topics that I could think about and relate to. I didn't know about those things or even know how to get myself a job.

REAL kept me strong and focused. Our meetings were a coming-together process. It helped me relate with another classmate, get knowledge from one another, and share information with each other. I guess you could say it was like a unit; we was doing things together. It taught me togetherness and how to work with people. That encouraged me to move on. I think that's what the program was really about—giving you courage and making you look at things from a different point of view, at least from a male's perspective anyway.

If it wasn't for REAL, I probably would have dropped out because I wasn't strong enough. And I think that goes for a lot of people that was in the same group as me. It helped to have an older male showing you responsibility, that you can still pass high school, you can still move on, and that it's ways around things—just showing you how to be a man and how to take care of yourself. REAL helped me a lot through those years. I needed that kind of guidance and knowledge that I could get from someone who could tell me about things. REAL made me want to get my diploma and get out.

I would say the best part of REAL that sticks out in my mind was when we were talking about how in college you should budget your money and watch yourself. Know your spending limit and know your saving limit. To this day, I still know how to budget my money. It's all up to me if I want to actually save my money or spend it. I realized the things that I need to pay for and the things that I don't need to pay for. What things I need to do and what things I don't need to do.

Another cool session was when were talking about females. We came up with thirty of today's harshest names for a female. I don't want to go down the list of names right now, but that activity was interesting. I ain't never really looked at society's view of women like that. For me to start looking at things and then realizing, made me think and it helped me out.

There wasn't much that I didn't like about REAL, except for near the end of my senior year when we wasn't really that organized. We were more organized in the beginning of 2000, the end of 2001. It flowed better. In my last year, it wasn't together as it should have been. That threw me off because we couldn't meet up or we'd have trouble finding a place for us all to talk, which the students didn't understand.

As far as the school, they really didn't seem to understand the kids, which is kind of bad. It should be about what the kids want. You gotta look at the kids. You're the principal and you know all about your boundaries or what you need to do, but what about the kids and how they feel about it? The teachers may have wanted the best for their students, but some of us didn't really feel it, especially with the whole Positive Living thing.

I know REAL, at that time, wasn't really that big, but the mentors were still trying to come up to the school and do this program for the kids. That's what first brung me to the program—them showing that they're interested and showing me different things. So for them being interested that made me want to see what's this program talking about.

But in the end, Visions made REAL an after-school program. And that didn't really work because people were trying to go home. REAL needs to be in school because that way you get all the students' attention and you won't have to deal with well, she's not coming or he's not coming because I know he's going to go home after school. So while it's in school and the school is still going, you can get all the students' attention that are in need of REAL.

I just want to thank Mr. Hall and all the founding members that were at REAL for showing me throughout those years the right roads and the wrong roads to take. They gave me guidance when I wasn't receiving guid-

ance at the time. I would like to thank all the members and the people
who stuck with me.

JAY GUEVARA

Jay Guevara, eighteen years old, enjoys playing basketball, drawing graffiti art, reading, and listening to all kinds of music. He says that music enhances his creativity, and he used that creativity to help produce and compose songs for the first REAL CD. Jay states, "Before, I used to listen to commercialized rap. But then, I started expanding and looking for other types of music like jazz, R&B, underground hip hop, techno. I listen to everything. There's something for every mood. Music is universal to me because it explains so much of my life and what I see and feel." Jay describes himself as passionate, social, and intelligent.

My full involvement with REAL started in 2000. This was also around the time when I was becoming more socially conscious about things. REAL was about looking at issues that plague the lives of African Americans, Latinos, the middle class, the lower class, and the lower-lower class. I know, when you start talking about social and ethnic issues, many people don't want to touch that with a twenty-foot pole. They tend to back away and just ignore it. But I liked it, and wanted to hear more of what Horace had to say.

Some of the topics that we talked about in meetings made me realize that there's more to the scenes that we see every day in our neighborhoods. Your friends are in gangs, but where do you think they're going to end up and why? Those types of questions and discussions had an impact on everyone's mind-set. Most people don't think or care about their consequences. Our discussions and activities made us more knowledgeable and helped to open our eyes to the world around us. It made us consider the other alternatives to the norm.

In our discussions, we learned to except other people's opinion, get an idea from that, learn, and grow together. You can refute an idea, but don't kill each other over it. Just learn to speak as a human being, person to person, man to man, and say, "You know this is what I think. What do

*you think about it?" The whole street bit isn't like that. Sometimes you
can't express your honest opinion because if someone disagrees, they have
no problem killing you. That's not about being man to man; that's about
being man to coward.*

*REAL wasn't about the whole street confrontation thing. Sure, we had
arguments because people are just going to disagree with you. But we still
came together on a common mission of becoming more socially conscious.
We looked at and examined our world more closely, realizing that we were
being fed garbage, but also realizing that we have the ability to rebel and
fight against it. Out of that, I made new friends. I built an association with
people that I probably wouldn't have done if we didn't have a place to
share our ideas. It was like a band, a group, a brotherhood, and that was
just one aspect of it. We got closer together, almost one, an entity. It came
naturally because of the way we could talk with each other and get respect
from each other.*

*REAL isn't just different from the streets; it's also different from regular
classes. Why? It's because you can escape to it. I know Jermaine felt that
way. He needed to escape from all the problems and the bullshit he had to
put up with. That's how I saw it and I think many of the guys saw it too.
It's a way to escape, relax, take a breather, and then go back to class, but
with a new train of thought about class work, homework, or a teacher you
couldn't stand. Once you got to the program, you could breathe, think,
and see that she [the teacher] is only doing her job and that you need to
do your job. If you don't, you may fail a test or not pass a class. Even
though I was an honor student, I still couldn't stand some of the people in
the classroom; I needed to get out. REAL was about letting me talk to my
boys, my people, the people who would listen to me. I could talk to them
about anything. Whether we were doing the Orlando Patterson type of
activities, talking about hip hop, or listening to music, it was a conversation period. From being around the guys, I appreciated my social personality a lot more, and that's good because 90 percent of life is dealing with
people.*

*I wish more kids could have experienced what I experienced in REAL.
Even though we had a large amount of the juniors, sophomores, and fresh-*

men, many of them were denied access by the administration. That, to me, was a shot in the foot. They had a program there that was a Band-Aid for the boys, and it ran from this time to this time. But when it came time to meet, the staff was like, "No. We can't let them go." So what was the entire freaking point of having this band-aid program when the teachers themselves were just poking more wounds into the males and letting them bleed and die in the classroom? There's the hypocrisy right there.

In fairness to the teachers, I think maybe some of the boys were unclear about what REAL was about. When our projects got out of the class, then maybe they wanted to get more involved, but they were still rather hesitant to do it because maybe they felt that they wouldn't fit in—an outsider kind of thing. I'm not sure. I still think that the biggest thing was the administration. More boys would have understood REAL if the administration had given it more support. When you have a smooth administration, you have a smooth program.

But let's get off of that and move on to the mentors of REAL. These guys fit my definition of mentoring, that is, the dissemination of knowledge from one person to the next. It's kind of like teaching, but it's not just about the books; it's about life. It's about the decisions one has made, whether it be the good side or the wrong side, and you pass that knowledge down so that someone can avoid that path or those negative situations. That's how I see it. Mentoring is a beautiful thing because you help shape and change one's life. REAL doesn't show one door; it shows all the doors. There's many ways to get where you want to go. And it's important to show all the doors because that leaves people with choices. Choices are important because what you do in the present becomes your future.

Basically, the mentors in the REAL are people who know what they're talking about. They exhibit what this program can help you to do. They have helped out a lot of us. Horace has helped out Jermaine. Cedrick has helped out me, Matthew, Lee, and Calvin. He's helped out the creative and music aspect of the program. Every mentor brings in their own quality and that's exactly how REAL is.

I find the REAL mentors to be supportive and understanding. This is important because I think when one takes a mentee, they just tend to think that they can just tell mentees what to do. Mentors need to be understanding of a mentee's knowledge. Know that a younger person is coming to you for your advice and wisdom because they don't know it. Mentors have to communicate with the person and just be themselves. Don't try to speak urban lingo if you don't know it. You just gotta find ways to relate to someone. Start off with communication and understanding. Communication is always the biggest because many things come out of it—intelligence, information sharing, and understanding. All that builds up to friendship.

About the Author

Horace R. Hall is a professor in the Department of Educational Policy Studies and Research at DePaul University in Chicago, Illinois. He teaches courses related to human development and learning, the philosophy and psychology of middle-level students, education and society, curriculum theorizing, and curriculum history. His present research interests and endeavors revolve around notions of identity formation, student empowerment and resilience, critical emancipatory teaching methods, and community social justice.

Prior to joining the faculty at DePaul University, Hall founded a grassroots community organization called REAL (Respect, Excellence, Attitude, and Leadership). As primarily a school-based mentoring program, REAL is designed to capture the attention of school-age youth by offering them a place to creatively express themselves through literacy, life skills, and arts-based curriculum. The idea for the REAL Youth Program was borne out of Hall's experiences as both a student and teacher in Chicago's public school system. Currently, Hall co-directs the program out of a host of public and charter schools in the Chicagoland area.